OPPOSING
VIEWPOINTS®
SERIES

Animal Experimentation

Other Books of Related Interest:

Opposing Viewpoints Series
Cloning

Ethics

Current Controversies Series
Medical Ethics

At Issue Series
Animal Experimentation

Do Animals Have Rights?

Prescription Drugs

"Congress shall make no law . . . abridging the freedom of speech, or of the press."

First Amendment to the U.S. Constitution

The basic foundation of our democracy is the First Amendment guarantee of freedom of expression. The Opposing Viewpoints Series is dedicated to the concept of this basic freedom and the idea that it is more important to practice it than to enshrine it.

OPPOSING VIEWPOINTS® SERIES

Animal Experimentation

David M. Haugen, Book Editor

GREENHAVEN PRESS

An imprint of Thomson Gale, a part of The Thomson Corporation

THOMSON
GALE

Detroit • New York • San Francisco • New Haven, Conn. • Waterville, Maine • London

Christine Nasso, *Publisher*
Elizabeth Des Chenes, *Managing Editor*

For more information, contact:
Greenhaven Press
27500 Drake Rd.
Farmington Hills, MI 48331-3535
Or you can visit our Internet site at http://www.gale.com

LIBRARY OF CONGRESS CATALOGING-IN-PUBLICATION DATA

Animal experimentation / David M. Haugen, book editor.
    p. cm. -- (Opposing viewpoints)
Includes bibliographical references and index.
ISBN-13: 978-0-7377-3346-4 (hardcover : alk. paper)
ISBN-10: 0-7377-3346-2 (hardcover : alk. paper)
ISBN-13: 978-0-7377-3347-1 (pbk. : alk. paper)
ISBN-10: 0-7377-3347-0 (pbk. : alk. paper)
1. Animal experimentation--Moral and ethical aspects. 2. Animal experimentation--United States. I. Haugen, David M., 1969–
    HV4915.A635 2006
    179'.4--dc22
                                                    2006031196

Contents

Why Consider Opposing Viewpoints?   11

Introduction   14

Chapter 1: Do Animals Have Rights?

Chapter Preface   21

1. Animals Have Rights   23
   Tom Regan

2. Animals Do Not Have Rights   29
   Ilana Mercer

3. Animals Are Equal to Humans   35
   Matt Ball and Jack Norris

4. Animals Are Not Equal to Humans   44
   Josie Appleton

5. Animal Rights Activists Are Terrorists   54
   Alex Epstein

6. Animal Rights Activists Are Not Terrorists   59
   Will Potter

7. Animal Researchers Should Not Be Bullied   64
   by Animal Rights Terrorists
   Fiona Fox

Periodical Bibliography   69

Chapter 2: Is Animal Experimentation Justifiable?

Chapter Preface   71

1. Animal Experimentation Is Ethical   73
   Adrian R. Morrison

2. Animal Experimentation Is Unethical   82
   David Thomas

3. Using Primates in Medical Experimentation   **102**
Is Justifiable
Scientific Steering Committee of the
European Commission

4. Using Primates in Medical Experimentation   **110**
Is Unjustifiable
John Gray

5. The Animal Experimentation Debate Has   **118**
Reached a Moral Deadlock
Peter Singer

6. The Moral Deadlock Concerning Animal   **124**
Experimentation Can Be Broken
Patrick Bateson

Periodical Bibliography   **134**

Chapter 3: Does Animal Experimentation Aid Medical Progress?

Chapter Preface   **136**

1. Animal Experimentation Is Vital to   **138**
Medical Research
American Physiological Society

2. Animal Experimentation Is Not Vital to   **144**
Medical Research
Christopher Anderegg et al.

3. Drug Testing on Animals Is Beneficial   **152**
Jennifer A. Hurley

4. Drug Testing on Animals Is Not Beneficial   **157**
Kathy Archibald

5. Microchip Technologies Could Make Drug   **165**
Testing on Animals Unnecessary
David H. Freedman

Periodical Bibliography   **173**

Chapter 4: Are New Forms of Animal Experimentation Worth Pursuing?

Chapter Preface   175

1. The Risks of Animal-to-Human Transplants   177
   Outweigh the Benefits
   Joyce D'Silva

2. The Benefits of Animal-to-Human   182
   Transplants Outweigh the Risks
   A physician, interviewed by Gale Scott

3. Genetically Modified Animals Are Beneficial   186
   to Medicine
   *Part I: Alexandre Fouassier, Part II:
   Manufacturing Chemist*

4. Genetically Modified Animals Are Not   192
   Beneficial to Medicine
   Animal Aid

5. Animal Cloning Is Worthwhile   197
   Marie A. Di Berardino

6. Animal Cloning Is Unnecessary   204
   Wayne Pacelle

Periodical Bibliography   209
For Further Discussion   210
Organizations to Contact   214
Bibliography of Books   221
Index   225

Why Consider Opposing Viewpoints?

> *"The only way in which a human being can make some approach to knowing the whole of a subject is by hearing what can be said about it by persons of every variety of opinion and studying all modes in which it can be looked at by every character of mind. No wise man ever acquired his wisdom in any mode but this."*
>
> *John Stuart Mill*

In our media-intensive culture it is not difficult to find differing opinions. Thousands of newspapers and magazines and dozens of radio and television talk shows resound with differing points of view. The difficulty lies in deciding which opinion to agree with and which "experts" seem the most credible. The more inundated we become with differing opinions and claims, the more essential it is to hone critical reading and thinking skills to evaluate these ideas. Opposing Viewpoints books address this problem directly by presenting stimulating debates that can be used to enhance and teach these skills. The varied opinions contained in each book examine many different aspects of a single issue. While examining these conveniently edited opposing views, readers can develop critical thinking skills such as the ability to compare and contrast authors' credibility, facts, argumentation styles, use of persuasive techniques, and other stylistic tools. In short, the Opposing Viewpoints Series is an ideal way to attain the higher-level thinking and reading skills so essential in a culture of diverse and contradictory opinions.

In addition to providing a tool for critical thinking, Opposing Viewpoints books challenge readers to question their own strongly held opinions and assumptions. Most people form their opinions on the basis of upbringing, peer pressure, and personal, cultural, or professional bias. By reading carefully balanced opposing views, readers must directly confront new ideas as well as the opinions of those with whom they disagree. This is not to simplistically argue that everyone who reads opposing views will—or should—change his or her opinion. Instead, the series enhances readers' understanding of their own views by encouraging confrontation with opposing ideas. Careful examination of others' views can lead to the readers' understanding of the logical inconsistencies in their own opinions, perspective on why they hold an opinion, and the consideration of the possibility that their opinion requires further evaluation.

Evaluating Other Opinions

To ensure that this type of examination occurs, Opposing Viewpoints books present all types of opinions. Prominent spokespeople on different sides of each issue as well as well-known professionals from many disciplines challenge the reader. An additional goal of the series is to provide a forum for other, less known, or even unpopular viewpoints. The opinion of an ordinary person who has had to make the decision to cut off life support from a terminally ill relative, for example, may be just as valuable and provide just as much insight as a medical ethicist's professional opinion. The editors have two additional purposes in including these less known views. One, the editors encourage readers to respect others' opinions—even when not enhanced by professional credibility. It is only by reading or listening to and objectively evaluating others' ideas that one can determine whether they are worthy of consideration. Two, the inclusion of such viewpoints encourages the important critical thinking skill of objectively evaluating an author's credentials and bias. This evaluation will illuminate an author's reasons for taking a particular stance on an issue and will aid in readers' evaluation of the author's ideas.

It is our hope that these books will give readers a deeper understanding of the issues debated and an appreciation of the complexity of even seemingly simple issues when good and honest people disagree. This awareness is particularly important in a democratic society such as ours in which people enter into public debate to determine the common good. Those with whom one disagrees should not be regarded as enemies but rather as people whose views deserve careful examination and may shed light on one's own.

Thomas Jefferson once said that "difference of opinion leads to inquiry, and inquiry to truth." Jefferson, a broadly educated man, argued that "if a nation expects to be ignorant and free . . . it expects what never was and never will be." As individuals and as a nation, it is imperative that we consider the opinions of others and examine them with skill and discernment. The Opposing Viewpoints Series is intended to help readers achieve this goal.

David L. Bender and Bruno Leone,
Founders

Introduction

> "No one can make an informed decision without free and open discussion. But how can you be informed if the people who have the information are threatened or even attacked whenever they speak out?"
>
> —Professor Steve Bloom,
> Hospital Doctor

> "Action is everything. Words and tears mean nothing to the animals trapped in their cages inside [Huntingdon Life Sciences] waiting to die. They deserve nothing less than our utmost commitment to take action every day to close down the lab that holds them captive and slowly kills them."
>
> —Stop Huntingdon Animal Cruelty
> Web site

Since the mid-1970s the Hall family of Staffordshire, England, had raised guinea pigs to supplement the earnings from their chief livelihood, sheep herding. The guinea pigs were sold to research laboratories that used them in various animal experiments. The added income helped the Halls' Darley Oaks Farm remain profitable throughout the 1980s and 1990s. But around 1999 the Halls' fortunes changed. Darley Oaks became the target of animal rights protesters who objected to the raising of guinea pigs for research. Over the next six years the Halls, their workers, and their business partners were subjected to taunts and scare tactics. As the British newsmagazine the *Economist* described in an August 2005 article,

[The Halls] have been abandoned by frightened suppliers and employees and lost their entire dairy herd, which was slaughtered when their tormentors made it impossible for the milk to be collected. The nadir came last year, when activists stole the body of Gladys Hammond, mother-in-law of one of the Hall brothers, from its grave in the churchyard at Yoxall in Staffordshire.

In hopes of regaining Gladys Hammond's remains and ending the terror campaign, the Hall family announced it would cease the breeding of guinea pigs for science.

The majority of animal rights protests have been vocal but peaceful, a trend that most animal rights spokespeople are quick to point out. In the past several years, however, the notoriety of a few campaigns involving intimidation and violence has captured the attention of the media, the scientific community, and the public in both England and the United States. Fear of the type of scare tactics experienced at Darley Oaks has influenced Cambridge University's decision to forgo plans to build a primate research facility, and Oxford University has been fighting in the courts to keep animal protesters from terrorizing contractors working on a new animal laboratory. Both English institutions have been the targets of organized rallies, and animal activist Web sites have published the names and addresses of university faculty, which Oxford authorities claim is an "incitement to harass" staff.

The most notable and sustained protest in recent years—one that has provided the impetus for the Oxford and Cambridge campaigns—has been the continuing demonstrations against Huntingdon Life Sciences, Europe's largest laboratory for conducting toxicity tests on animals. Huntingdon performs about seventy-five thousand toxicity tests each year. The animals used in such tests are primarily rodents, but a few hundred dogs and primates are also part of Huntingdon's testing procedures. Animal rights groups began targeting Huntingdon Life Sciences (then Huntingdon Research Centre) in the late 1980s after an activist infiltrated the labs and exposed the rough treatment of animals, poor caging facilities, and the grim reality of toxicity testing. The story broke in 1989 and garnered much public sympathy but no official sanctions for the lab. Subsequent infiltrations in the late 1990s supplied some filmed abuse of dogs that was aired on British television. In response, two animal activists formed Stop Huntingdon Animal Cruelty (SHAC), a British organization—with international support—aimed at shutting down Huntingdon Life Sciences.

Since its founding SHAC has come under fire for exceeding the bounds of peaceful protest. Death threats, vandalism, and false bomb threats have been linked to SHAC's campaign against Huntingdon employees. According to the Victims of Animal Rights Extremism Web site, one computer scientist at Huntingdon wrote of his experience:

> I recently woke up to find two of my cars trashed and the graffiti "puppy killers" sprayed on the side of one of them. They had punctured two tyres. One car was effectively written off. There were slogans sprayed on my house. . . . That in itself was bad enough but over the weekend my name, address and telephone number went up on the SHAC website, which was effectively inviting local activists to come and have a go.

> Besides targeting employees, SHAC has also been accused of intimidating suppliers and contractors working with Huntingdon Life Sciences. These efforts have been so successful that prominent financial backers have pulled their interests out of the corporation.

The unparalleled efforts of SHAC and other animal rights organizations operating in the United Kingdom have brought about some reaction from authorities. In April 2005 the British Parliament passed the Serious Organised Crime and Police Act, which, in part, makes it illegal to harass people at their homes or to cause interference in business concerns as part of a demonstration. One result of the British law was to quell some of the terror tactics at home while simultaneously igniting them overseas. Protests of Huntingdon Life Sciences lab facilities in New Jersey began to swell in the new millennium after SHAC's unusual brand of dissent showed results in Britain. Kevin Kjonaas, the twenty-eight-year-old president of SHAC USA, the U.S. counterpart of Stop Huntingdon Animal Cruelty, organized protests outside employees' homes and allowed the posting of employees' phone numbers and addresses, as well as the names of their children, on the SHAC USA Web site.

Like Britain, the United States has laws meant to curb intimidation campaigns. Originally passed in 1992 and strengthened after the September 11, 2001, terrorist attacks, the Animal Enterprise Protection Act protects animal testing institutions and their employees. In May 2004, Kjonaas and six other SHAC members were indicted under the act primarily for what the government calls an Internet fear campaign. As reported in a January 2006 issue of *Mother Jones*, "John Lewis, the FBI's deputy assistant director for counterterrorism, told Congress . . . that SHAC and other animal rights groups represent America's No. 1 domestic terror threat."

The trial of Kjonaas and his colleagues in the United States as well as the conflict that still rages in England reveal the extremes reached in the debate over animal experimentation. Defenders of animal research claim that animals provide the best nonhuman testing models for determining the risks of new drugs and medical treatments. Using animals in experiments will also increase the understanding of human and animal physiology and psychology, advocates say. Such arguments are embraced by a large percentage of the scientific community. In a 2004 issue of *Hospital Doctor*, Professor Tipu Aziz of University of Oxford and Imperial College London encouraged scientists to speak out against intimidation by animal activists. He told his peers, "Anyone who has been to medical school and treated patients will understand the vital contribution made by animal research."

Detractors, however, tell a different story. Many believe animal research has never influenced the great medical discoveries of the past and is not likely to do so in the future. They argue that animals do not provide proper models for human physiology, and therefore any drug testing or other experiments cannot provide results that would translate to humans. Animal activists, such as those involved with the fight against Huntingdon Life Sciences, also contend that it is unethical to treat animals as a means to human ends. These activists assert that the pain and suffering experienced by test animals should not be tolerated by any empathetic and reasonable person. University lecturer Sharon Howe wrote in a March 2006 editorial to the *Independent* (a UK newspaper), "How can painfully and artificially inducing human diseases in other species with a different genetic make-up to our own possibly advance the cause of modern medicine?"

The impassioned arguments of animal activists coupled with evidence of inhumane treatment of animals at some research institutions have already brought about legislation in many countries that subjects animal experimentation to rigorous government oversight and inspection. In addition, the scientific community subscribes to a belief that reducing the need for animal experiments by replacing these tests with other types of experiments (computer modeling, for example) is a worthy goal. Taken together, these factors have consistently and drastically cut the number of animal experiments performed throughout the world since the 1970s. However, to animal rights advocates, reduction is not enough, and this belief has led to the extremist actions making headlines in recent years.

Although the lawyer for Kevin Kjonaas and his six colleagues was reported in the *New York Times* as stating, "Advocating obnoxiously is not a crime," the courts have already decided otherwise. In March 2006 six of the seven convicted members of SHAC USA were found guilty by a federal jury and face maximum sentences ranging from three to five years' imprisonment and up to $250,000 in fines. The guilty verdict, however, has not stopped the protests, and the debate over the supposed terrorist actions of some animal rights groups continues. This controversy is one of many deliberated in the chapter Do Animals Have Rights? in *Animal Experimentation: Opposing Viewpoints*. Other chapters in this anthology ask the following questions: Is Animal Experimentation Justifiable? Does Animal Experimentation Aid Medical Progress? Are New Forms of Animal Experimentation Worth Pursuing? These chapters lay out the fundamental questions that surround animal experimentation, a contentious issue that has prompted reasoned debate as well as intimidation and criminal behavior.

|Do Animals Have Rights?

Chapter Preface

In a July 2000 essay, Tibor Machan, a professor of business ethics, points out that animals are sometimes driven by instinct to kill their own offspring. Fish, he notes, occasionally eat their young, and lions often slaughter chosen cubs. Although Machan acknowledges that the reasons for this are not clear, he states that the conduct is a matter of "genetic disposition." Why then, he asks, are humans subject to criminal prosecution if they engaged in similar behavior?

Machan's question strikes at the heart of the controversy over animal rights. Those, like Machan, who believe there is a fundamental difference between animals and humans contend that the concept of "rights" cannot apply to creatures that are driven primarily by instinct. On the other hand, humans, Machan says, "have the capacity to make choices, they possess free will and have the responsibility to act ethically and respect the rights of other human beings. . . . Human beings, in short, are free and morally responsible. And it is this fact that gives rise to their having basic rights that others ought to respect and they may protect with force and law."

Critics of Machan's argument, however, insist that animals need not be granted rights by humans. To them, people and animals possess natural rights to share the planet and live freely. Some animal rights advocates also claim that human morality approves of the concept of animal rights. They contend that moral principles are based on the capacity to suffer because it is the only ethically relevant standard that is common to all people. These critics charge that because people would be acting immorally if they caused suffering to others, then they are acting immorally if they cause suffering to animals. For this reason, people should refrain from using animals to their own ends—especially in scientific experiments in which animals are made to suffer to advance human knowledge. Or more broadly, as the international animal rights group Animal Liberation argues: "Animals may not be killed, exploited, cruelly treated, intimidated, or imprisoned for no good reason. Animals should be able to live in peace, according to their own needs and preferences."

Some of the authors in the following chapter debate whether animals possess rights and whether these rights or the inherent worth of animals should deter people from using them in scientific experimentation. Other authors represented in this chapter extend this argument to question whether there are limits on how far champions of animal rights should go in carrying out what they see as a moral duty to protect animal interests.

> *"There is no 'superior' species. To think otherwise is to be no less prejudiced than racists or sexists."*

Animals Have Rights

Tom Regan

Tom Regan is an emeritus professor of philosophy at North Carolina State University and the author of The Case for Animal Rights. *In the following viewpoint, Regan explains why animals should be afforded the same rights claimed by humans. He argues that it is just and ethical to concede rights to animals because to treat animals with less respect than humans is speciesism—a form of prejudice. People should protect and defend animals, Regan states, because animals cannot speak up for themselves. If humans wish to live up to their ethical natures, he insists, then they should act with compassion; they should recognize that animals have inherent worth and are not commodities to be used.*

As you read, consider the following questions:

1. In Regan's view, what is the highest principle of ethics? How does he apply this principle to the case for animal rights?

Tom Regan, "The Philosophy of Animal Rights," The Culture & Animals Foundation, 1997. www.cultureandanimals.org. Reproduced by permission.

2. What four things do all ethical philosophies emphasize, according to Regan?

3. In the author's view, how is animal exploitation connected to environmental degradation?

It is not rational to discriminate arbitrarily. And discrimination against nonhuman animals is arbitrary. It is wrong to treat weaker human beings, especially who are lacking in normal human intelligence, as "tools" or "renewable resources" or "models" or "commodities." It cannot be right, therefore, to treat other animals as if they were "tools," "models" and the like, if their psychology is as rich as (or richer than) these humans. To think otherwise is irrational.

The Philosophy of Animal Rights Is Scientific

The philosophy of animal rights is respectful of our best science in general and evolutionary biology in particular. The latter teaches that, in Darwin's words, humans differ from many other animals "in degree, not in kind." Questions of line drawing to one side, it is obvious that the animals used in laboratories, raised for food, and hunted for pleasure or trapped for profit, for example, are our psychological kin. This is no fantasy, this is fact, proven by our best science.

The Philosophy of Animal Rights Is Unprejudiced

Racists are people who think that the members of their race are superior to the members of other races simply because the former belong to their (the "superior") race. Sexists believe that the members of their sex are superior to the members of the opposite sex simply because the former belong to their (the "superior") sex. Both racism and sexism are paradigms of unsupportable bigotry. There is no "superior" or "inferior" sex or race. Racial and sexual differences are biological, not moral, differences.

So Close to Human

To people used to dividing the world up into "humans" and "animals" it comes as a shock to realise that the genetic differences between humans and chimpanzees are smaller than those between chimpanzees and gorillas. . . . Why, then, do we continue to insist that even the most basic rights, like those to life, liberty and protection from torture, are for humans only?

Peter Singer, "Some Are More Equal,"
Guardian *(UK), May 19, 2003.*

The same is true of speciesism—the view that members of the species *Homo sapiens* are superior to members of every other species simply because human beings belong to one's own (the "superior") species. For there is no "superior" species. To think otherwise is to be no less prejudiced than racists or sexists.

The Philosophy of Animal Rights Is Just

Justice is the highest principle of ethics. We are not to commit or permit injustice so that good may come, not to violate the rights of the few so that the many might benefit. Slavery allowed this. Child labor allowed this. Most examples of social injustice allow this. But not the philosophy of animal rights, whose highest principle is that of justice: No one has a right to benefit as a result of violating another's rights, whether that "other" is a human being or some other animal.

The Philosophy of Animal Rights Is Compassionate

A full human life demands feelings of empathy and sympathy—in a word, compassion—for the victims of injustice—whether the victims are humans or other animals. The philosophy of animal rights calls for, and its acceptance fosters the growth of, the virtue of compassion. This philosophy is, in [Abraham] Lincoln's words, "the way of a whole human being."

The Philosophy of Animal Rights Is Unselfish

The philosophy of animal rights demands a commitment to serve those who are weak and vulnerable—those who, whether they are humans or other animals, lack the ability to speak for or defend themselves, and who are in need of protection against human greed and callousness. This philosophy requires this commitment, not because it is in our self-interest to give it, but because it is right to do so. This philosophy therefore calls for, and its acceptance fosters the growth of, unselfish service.

The Philosophy of Animal Rights Is Individually Fulfilling

All the great traditions in ethics, both secular and religious, emphasize the importance of four things: knowledge, justice, compassion, and autonomy. The philosophy of animal rights is no exception. This philosophy teaches that our choices should be based on knowledge, should be expressive of compassion and justice, and should be freely made. It is not easy to achieve these virtues, or to control the human inclinations toward greed and indifference. But a whole human life is impossible without them. The philosophy of animal rights both calls for, and its acceptance fosters the growth of, individual self-fulfillment.

The Philosophy of Animal Rights Is Socially Progressive

The greatest impediment to the flourishing of human society is the exploitation of other animals at human hands. This is true in the case of unhealthy diets, of the habitual reliance on the "whole animal model" in science, and of the many other forms animal exploitation takes. And it is no less true of education and advertising, for example, which help deaden the human psyche to the demands of reason, impartiality, compassion, and justice. In all these ways (and more), nations remain profoundly backward because they fail to serve the true interests of their citizens.

The Philosophy of Animal Rights Is Environmentally Wise

The major cause of environmental degradation, including the greenhouse effect, water pollution, and the loss both of arable land and top soil, for example, can be traced to the exploitation of animals. This same pattern exists throughout the broad range of environmental problems, from acid rain and ocean dumping of toxic wastes, to air pollution and the destruction of natural habitat. In all these cases, to act to protect the affected animals (who are, after all, the first to suffer and die from these environmental ills), is to act to protect the earth.

The Philosophy of Animal Rights Is Peace-Loving

The fundamental demand of the philosophy of animal rights is to treat humans and other animals with respect. To do this requires that we not harm anyone just so that we ourselves or others might benefit. This philosophy therefore is totally opposed to military aggression. It is a philosophy of peace. But it is a philosophy that extends the demand for peace beyond the boundaries of our species. For there is a war being waged, every day, against countless millions of nonhuman animals. To stand truly for peace is to stand firmly against speciesism. It is wishful thinking to believe that there can be "peace in the world" if we fail to bring peace to our dealings with other animals.

We and They Are Equal

We are not saying that humans and other animals are equal in every way. For example, we are not saying that dogs and cats can do calculus, or that pigs and cows enjoy poetry. What we are saying is that, like humans, many other animals are psychological beings, with an experiential welfare of their own. In this sense, we and they are the same. In this sense, therefore, despite our many differences, we and they are equal.

I *"The nature of animals makes them worthy of human compassion, kindness and care, but never of any human rights."*

Animals Do Not Have Rights

Ilana Mercer

In the following viewpoint, Ilana Mercer claims that people have a distorted view of animal nature. Instead of recognizing that animals have no conscience and act out of instinct, many people tend to treat animals as rational creatures with near-human attributes. According to Mercer, this has prompted activists to suggest that animals are deserving of the same rights possessed by humans. Such a view is unfounded, Mercer says, because rights only exist among moral beings with the capacity to reason. Animals, therefore, can be worthy of human compassion but could never possess human rights. Ilana Mercer is an analyst for the Internet's Free Market News Network and the author of Broad Sides: One Woman's Clash with a Corrupt Culture.

As you read, consider the following questions:

1. In Mercer's examples, how has the media altered people's perceptions of animals?

2. How does Mercer counter the argument that some primates deserve rights because they are genetically similar to humans?

3. According to the author, from what two attributes are human rights derived?

A vague anxiety underlies the media's preoccupation with the recent attacks on people by predators—Roy Horn of the "Siegfried and Roy" act was mauled by a tiger, and grizzly-bear advocate Timothy Treadwell and his companion were gobbled up in Alaska while traveling across bear country (without weapons).

As more wild animals brazenly make themselves at home in manicured suburbs, people, including media top dogs, worry. And for good reason. They are taught from cradle to crypt that humans have encroached on the animals' territory. On television, "Animal Planet" *experts* tell them (mostly incorrectly) how rare, essential to the "ecosystem," and misunderstood these creatures are.

Equally unassailable is the premise that you don't shoot alligators, bears, coyotes and cougars—not even when they threaten hearth and home. Should a "situation" arise, to avoid criminal charges, one is expected to practically Mirandize the animal [read it its criminal rights] before eliminating it.

[Television commentator] Bill O'Reilly conducted a species-sensitive interview with a couple of animal trainers following Horn's mauling. The urban legend now making the rounds has it that, after being reluctantly dragged by the animal to a more secluded picnic spot, Horn, a jet of blood squirting from his neck, told paramedics not to kill the tiger.

Well, perhaps. But Roy need not have worried his poor—and by then also poorly attached—head. The O'Reilly interview was marked by the same forlorn fatalism. The typical PETA-friendly (People for the Ethical Treatment of Animals) discussion, replete with anthropomorphism (the practice of attributing human characteristics to an animal) followed. Everyone agreed solemnly that the animal didn't intend to commit a crime.

Animals Act Without Conscience

Forgive me if this is too (excuse the expression) catty a point to make, but isn't that the case with creatures that have no capacity for conscious thought? Unlike human beings, animals are incapable of forming malicious intent—they simply act reflexively, in a stimulus-response manner.

Because animals kill with no forethought or conscience, we don't hold them responsible for their actions in the legal sense, as we would a human being. We agree they were only acting on their animal instincts—they don't function on a higher plane.

Yet a public long fed a diet of Disneyfied cartoon animals has also swallowed a lot of pabulum about the "humanness" of animals. We've reached the point that even quasi-scientific National Geographic may give Christian names to its boa constrictor film stars. As the animal slithers on its random way, the creepy narrator will also imbue the creature with elaborate inner concerns. In the event that this curdled schmaltz fails to sicken viewers, it should, at the very least, have the credibility of a "Winnie the Pooh" overdub.

Not Moral Beings

Animal-rights advocates—some of whom even walk upright and have active frontal lobes—argue, for instance, that because the great apes share a considerable portion of our genetic material, they are just like human beings, and ought to be given human rights.

As of yet, though, Alexei A. Abrikosov, Vitaly L. Ginzburg and Anthony J. Leggett are not the names of lower primates—they are the names of the 2003 Nobel Prize winners in phys-

Animals Have a Fixed Value

Animals never have any potential to do anything greater than their ancestors and direct contemporaries. Animals are not individual because while they may have distinct characteristics they lack the capacity to develop themselves and transform their existence. Animals are also not social because while they may live within groups, they lack the capacity to transform that group's behavior and they cannot take collective decisions within the group. In this sense, the value of animals is fixed such that it is always comparable to any other animal currently living, dead or projected into the future.

Stuart Derbyshire, speech given at the Edinburgh (Scotland) Book Festival, August 19, 2002.

ics. No matter how many genes these men share with monkeys and no matter how sentient chimps are, the latter will never contribute anything to "the theory of superconductors and superfluids," or author a document like the "Declaration of Independence," much less tell good from bad.

Given that human beings are so vastly different in mental and moral stature from apes, the lesson from any genetic similarities the species share is this and no more: A few genes are responsible for very many incalculable differences!

Unlike human beings, animals by their nature are not moral agents. They possess no free will, no capacity to tell right from wrong, and cannot reflect on their actions. While they often act quite wonderfully, their motions are merely a matter of conditioning.

Since man is a rational agent, with the gift of consciousness and a capacity to scrutinize his deeds and chart his actions, we hold him culpable for his transgressions. A human being's exceptional ability to discern right from wrong makes him punishable for any criminal depravity.

Animals Have No Claim to Rights

Man's nature is the source of the responsibility he bears for his actions. It is also the source of his rights. Human or individual rights, such as the rights to life, liberty and property, are derived from man's innate moral agency and capacity for reason.

Unfortunately, the new-generation, campy "conservatives," who look to Bo Derek as the Republican brain trust on animal rights, desperately need an explanation of what a right is.

A right is a legal claim against another. As author and lecturer Robert Bidinotto points out in his manifesto against environmentalism and animal rights, rights establish boundaries among those who possess them. Since animals can't recognize such boundaries, they should certainly not be granted legal powers against human beings.

Moreover, the rights human beings possess exist within the context of a moral community. Animals don't belong to a moral community—they answer the call of the wild. When a simian devours her young ones, none of her sisters in the colony hoot a la [animal activist and scientist] Jane Goodall for justice. Not one of the many tigers lounging around on Siegfried and Roy's Little Bavaria estate is catcalling for the majestic head of their errant teammate.

The nature of animals makes them worthy of human compassion, kindness and care, but never of any human rights.

The perverse, pagan, public theatre elicited by animal attacks ought to give way to some life-loving, logical lessons. It is in the nature of things for predators to kill. Wild animals have big pointy teeth for a reason, wrote John Robson of the *Ottawa Citizen*.

A civilized society places human life above all else and endorses its vigorous defense—it doesn't show resignation when beast attacks man.

In the future, if a working wild animal repeats this perfectly predictable performance, a stage hand should be poised to lodge a bullet in the critter's skull. The same goes for bears in the backyard.

> *"If animals can feel pain as humans can, and desire to live as humans do, how can we deny them similar respect?"*

Animals Are Equal to Humans

Matt Ball and Jack Norris

In the following selection, Matt Ball and Jack Norris insist that arguments against granting rights to animals are flawed. The authors claim that the only ethical criterion that should determine whether creatures should have rights is their capacity to suffer. If animals can suffer, the authors assert, then they have a subjective desire to survive, and therefore they deserve the right to pursue life. Humans cannot overlook this fact if they wish to maintain a consistent and equitable standard of morality, Ball and Norris conclude. Matt Ball is the cofounder and executive director of Vegan Outreach, an animal rights organization. Jack Norris is the president of Vegan Outreach.

As you read, consider the following questions:

1. According to Ball and Norris, why is it unsound to deny animals rights on the basis of lower intelligence and lack of technological advancement?

Matt Ball and Jack Norris, "Beyond Might Makes Right," Vegan Outreach, n.d. www. veganoutreach.org. Reproduced by permission.

2. How does the concept of "subjective experience" factor into the authors' argument about why animals should have rights?

3. As cited in the article, how have Carl Sagan and Ann Druyan illustrated that animals may be moral beings?

In most of the world, human beings are granted basic rights. These fundamental rights are usually (at a minimum): the entitlement of individuals to have basic control of their lives and bodies, without infringing on the rights of others. In other words: the right not to be killed, caged, or experimented on against their will at the hands of moral agents (persons able to understand and act from a moral code). It is assumed that the reader believes humans to have these rights.

A Difference of Degree

Many say that humans deserve rights while other animals do not because humans have a greater level of certain characteristics: humans are more intelligent, creative, aware, technologically advanced, dominant able to use language, able to enter into contracts, able to make moral choices, etc. Thus, humans deserve rights because they have a greater degree of these characteristics.

This argument has two problems:

- Rights are not relevant to a group (e.g., "humans"), but only to individuals. Individuals, not groups, are exploited and are capable of suffering and dying; individuals, not groups, are denied rights when there is a morally relevant reason (e.g., after committing a crime).

- Not all humans possess these characteristics to a greater degree than all other non-humans. There are non-humans who are more intelligent, creative, aware, dominant, technologically advanced (in reference to tool making), and able to use language, than some humans (such as infants or severely handicapped humans). Furthermore, many animals perform actions that, in humans, would be labeled moral behavior; oftentimes some animals act more ethically than many humans. If rights were granted at a certain threshold of intelligence, creativity, moral behavior, etc., some animals would have rights and some humans would not.

Value to Others

Some say that even though infants do not possess high levels of some characteristics, they should be granted rights because they are valued by other humans (their parents, for instance). By this argument, infants themselves do not possess any inherent rights, but receive them only if valued by an adult human.

At the same time, being valued by an adult human does not grant rights to pigs, parakeets, pet rocks, or Porsches. This is inconsistent: either one is granted rights by being valued by an adult human—and thus everything valued by an adult human has rights—or there must be different criteria for granting rights. . . .

Biological Rights

Another argument is that humans have rights because they belong to the species Homo sapiens. In other words, a chimpanzee may very well be as intelligent (or creative, etc.) as some humans, but chimpanzees do not have rights because they are not members of the biologically-defined rights-bearing species, Homo sapiens.

In the past, there have been a number of biological definitions of what constitutes a species. Today, it is defined genetically. The questions then become:

- Why should rights be deserved solely on the basis of a certain arrangement of genes?

- Among the genes that determine one's eye color, etc. which gene is it that confers rights?

- If rights should be based on genes, why should the line be drawn at the species level? Why shouldn't the line be drawn at race, order, phylum, or kingdom?

A thoughtful person might find having their rights (or lack thereof) determined by a molecular sequence to be a bit absurd. It is no better than basing rights on the pigmentation of one's skin (which is also determined by the individual's genetic code). . . .

The Golden Rule

In the past, humans may have respected each other's rights in order to survive without constant violence. Many people still function on this level. Yet over time, more civilized people have evolved a moral system that grants rights not just based on self-protection but on the Golden Rule—treat your neighbor as you would like to be treated. We know that we want to stay alive, do not wish to suffer, etc., and we assume others like us have the same desires. Being capable of looking beyond our own individual interests we apply the Golden Rule even to people who could not harm us.

How much like us do beings have to be before we include them under the Golden Rule? At one time, women were not enough like the men who held power to be granted many rights. Neither were minorities in the United States and other societies. Even though the circle has expanded to include these individuals in the United States, today other animals are still not considered sufficiently like us for the majority of people to treat these animals as our neighbors under the Golden Rule.

The Soul

Some would say having a God-given soul is what gives one rights. There is no way to prove that humans have souls, just

"Well, if—as everyone insists—we've a superior social organisation, communications system, ecological sense and an ability to adjust, how is it we're becoming extinct?"

Ed Fisher. © Punch Rothco. Reproduced by permission.

as there is no way to prove that all other animals lack souls. Those who insist that only humans have souls (and thus rights) are faced with a theological dilemma: it would require a cruel God to create beings with the capacity to feel pain and the desire to live, if these animals' purpose was to suffer at the hands of humans.

Animals Kill Each Other

Some defend humans killing animals on the grounds that animals kill each other in nature. These people would be hard pressed to show that our modern systems of animal agriculture or experimentation are "natural."

While it is true that some animals kill other animals in nature, moral philosophy is based on principles, not excused by the actions of others. As [animal activist and scholar] Peter Singer writes: "You cannot evade responsibility by imitating beings who are incapable of making [an ethical] choice." Some humans assault, rape, or kill other humans, yet we do not condone these actions. . . .

Suffering Is the Criterion

Searching for some characteristic to justify granting rights to all humans while denying rights to all other animals is futile. A moral system based on any of the characteristics discussed so far would either include many non-human animals or exclude some humans.

To have a consistent set of ethics a characteristic must be found that not only allows for the inclusion of all humans, but is also morally relevant. The only characteristic that simply and consistently meets these requirements is the capacity for suffering.

As Jeremy Bentham, head of the Department of Jurisprudence at Oxford University during the 19th century, said in reference to his belief that animals should be granted moral consideration, "The question is not, Can they reason? nor, 'Can they talk?' But rather, 'Can they suffer?'"

If a thing cannot suffer, then it does not matter to that being what happens to it. For example, computers have forms of intelligence (in many ways greater than that of any human), but these machines do not care whether they are turned off or even destroyed.

On the other hand, if a being is able to have subjective experiences of pleasure and pain, then it does matter—to that individual—what happens to it. Irrespective of intelligence, language, etc., a conscious, sentient being has interests in its existence—at the very least to avoid pain and to stay alive. Any complete ethic cannot ignore these concerns.

For the Love of Animals

There are many who claim that they love animals and don't want them to suffer. Few oppose "humane" treatment of animals. But fewer still are willing to give up their prejudice of human superiority. Thus, the distance between the acceptable treatment and the actual, institutionalized treatment of these animals is greater than ever: slaughterhouses are hidden away from populated areas, and vivisectors' labs are closed and locked.

Many scientists claim they use animals only when it is "absolutely necessary to save human lives." Ignoring the question of whether or not their contention of necessity is accurate and what is the ethical use of limited resources for medical care and research, these people are betrayed by their actions: how many vegetarian vivisectors are there? They can hardly argue that it is necessary for them to kill animals for food.

In general, the animal welfarist position, which has been endorsed (but sparsely adopted) by the meat industry and pro-vivisection groups, is at odds with a truly respectful relationship based on the recognition of the rights of other animals. Welfarists concede that animals have interests, but these animals remain human property. Thus, the fundamental interests of the animals remain secondary to any interests of the owners. Laws based on the welfarist position, such as the federal Animal Welfare Act, have proven to be almost useless in every practical sense as any use/abuse of an animal is allowed if deemed "necessary".

Trying to legislate a humane balance between the interests of animals and the interests of humans sounds good in principle and appeals to most. However, given that the current system still allows such atrocities as canned hunts, castration without anesthesia, factory farms, pain experiments, etc., animal abuse will continue until the current system recognizes that many animals are conscious, sentient beings whose rights are independent of the interests of humans. . . .

Even though rights can only be granted consistently and justly on the basis of the capacity to suffer and not on the ability to make moral choices, there is ample evidence that many animals can and do make moral choices, often to the shame of "superior" humans. As Drs. Carl Sagan and Ann Druyan relate in *Shadows of Forgotten Ancestors*:

> In the annals of primate ethics, there are some accounts that have the ring of parable. In a laboratory setting, macaques were fed if they were willing to pull a chain and electrically shock an unrelated macaque whose agony was in plain view through a one-way mirror. Otherwise, they starved. After learning the ropes, the monkeys frequently refused to pull the chain: in one experiment only 13% would do so—87% preferred to go hungry. One macaque went without food for nearly two weeks rather than hurt its fellow. Macaques who had themselves been shocked in previous experiments were even less willing to pull the chain. The relative social status or gender of the macaques had little bearing on their reluctance to hurt others.

If asked to choose between the human experimenters offering the macaques this Faustian bargain and the macaques themselves—suffering from real hunger rather than causing pain to others—our own moral sympathies do not lie with the scientists. But their experiments permit us to glimpse in non-humans a saintly willingness to make sacrifices in order to save others—even those who are not close kin. By conventional human standards, these macaques—who have never gone to Sunday school, never heard of the Ten Commandments, never squirmed through a single junior high school civics lesson—seem exemplary in their moral grounding and their courageous resistance to evil. Among these macaques, at least in this case, heroism is the norm. If the circumstances were reversed, and captive humans were offered the same deal by macaque scientists, would we do as well? (Especially when there is an authority figure urging us to administer the electric shocks, we humans are disturbingly willing to cause pain—and for a reward much more paltry than food is for a starving macaque.) In human history there are a precious few whose memory we revere because they knowingly sacrificed themselves for others. For each of them, there are multitudes who did nothing.

If animals can feel pain as humans can, and desire to live as humans do, how can we deny them similar respect? As moral beings, how can we justify our continued exploitation of them?

We must stand up against the idea that might makes right. We must question the status quo which allows the unquestioned infliction of so much suffering. We must act from our own ethics, rather than blindly follow authority figures who tell us it's okay and even necessary to harm animals.

Discussing the macaque monkeys who chose to starve rather than inflict pain on another, Drs. Sagan and Druyan conclude, "Might we have a more optimistic view of the human future if we were sure our ethics were up to their standards?"

> *"Humans are the measure of all things: morality starts with us."*

Animals Are Not Equal to Humans

Josie Appleton

Josie Appleton is an assistant editor for Spiked, *an Internet newsmagazine. In the following selection, Appleton argues against the notion that animals and humans are morally or otherwise equal. Appleton states that enlightened human thought has consistently disproved such equality, maintaining instead that humans are superior due to their rational and ethical capacities. Humans, Appleton points out, possess a consciousness—not merely an instinct—that allows for self-reflection and the ability to develop civilizations. Because animals can never acquire such traits, they could never be the equal to humans.*

As you read, consider the following questions:

1. According to Appleton, why does German philosopher Immanuel Kant argue that it is ethical for humans to use animals for their own interests?

2. In Appleton's view, what has been Christianity's stance on the relationship between animals and humans?

Josie Appleton, "Speciesism: A Beastly Concept," *Spiked*, February 23, 2006. www.spiked-online.com. © 2006 *Spiked*. All rights reserved. Reproduced by permission.

3. Referring to evolution, how does the author illustrate that the distinction between animals and humans is one of "kind" and not "degree"?

[In his 1977 book. *Animal Liberation*] Animal rights activist Peter Singer defines speciesism as 'a prejudice or attitude of bias towards the interests of members of one's own species and against those of members of other species'. Advocates argue that fighting speciesism is an extension of struggles for human equality: just as we once dehumanised others on the basis of their race or sex, so apparently we now think animals are below us. The argument goes that speciesism, racism and sexism are all examples of 'exclusionary attitudes'. In *The Political Animal: The Conquest of Speciesism*, Richard Ryder notes that Aristotle thought that animals 'exist for the sake of men' while also looking down on slaves and women. No coincidence, says Ryder. According to Ryder, either you are a caring person who recognises the value of other beings, or you are selfish and care only for yourself. He cites 'evidence of a link between caring for humans and caring for animals': one study found that opponents of animal rights tended to be male, anti-abortion, have 'prejudice against homosexuals' and 'exhibited racial prejudice'; another study of US students concluded that 'those students who favour animal experimentation tend to be male, masculine in outlook, conservative and less empathetic'. . . .

The term speciesism hasn't yet entered the popular vocabulary, perhaps partly because it is such a mouthful. But the assumption behind the term—that it is wrong to prioritise humans over animals—has become mainstream. . . . Of course, in practice most of us are speciesist: we eat animals but not humans; we buy pets and keep them locked up in cages; we support animal experimentation in order to save human lives. But increasingly these distinctions lack moral justification. It's time we developed a more human-centred morality, to provide our practical judgements with intellectual support.

Changing Notions of Human and Animal Equality

Animal rights activists get the relationship between human and animal equality completely skewed. In actual fact, the idea of the brotherhood of mankind was founded on the basis of uniquely human features. In the Enlightenment, when the notion of human equality was hammered out, it was argued that we should treat one another as equals because we were all rational, self-conscious beings. The German philosopher Immanuel Kant argued that we have to respect other human beings because they are *self-willing*: they are conscious of their existence, so you cannot merely treat them as a means to your end. By contrast, says Kant, 'Animals are not self-conscious and are there merely as a means to an end. That end is man'. It is because animals are not ends for themselves that humans can treat them as a means to our ends.

The flowering of human consciousness went hand-in-hand with a growing distinction from animals. It is when humans lived in cramped and degraded circumstances that they have felt the most commonality with the beasts. In ancient Egypt, cats and dogs were mummified because they were believed to have an afterlife, and Egyptian Gods had animal heads. Premodern societies often had animal totems, and they saw animals and humans as intertwined through reincarnation. Animals were attributed with agency: some societies tried animals in court, and prayed to fish to return to the rivers. The sense of fellowship with animals corresponded to societies subject to the whims of nature. These circumstances didn't foster brotherly love. . . .

With Ancient Greece, when humanity began to develop a fuller sense of itself and its abilities, animals began to be cast out of the picture. Greek Gods are all human—though they sometimes disguise themselves as animals, as in the myth of Leda and the swan. Human-animal hybrids remained in the form of satyrs and mermaids, but crucially these had human heads and arms and so retained the locus of personality. Theorists of ethics and the good life, such as Aristotle, generally argued that animals lacked reason and so could not be granted justice.

A Clearer Distinction Between Human and Animal

Christianity developed a broader notion of human equality, and a clearer distinction between humans and animals. We are all made in the image of God, says the Bible, even women and slaves, and we are all deserving of equal respect. Christianity respected no holy animals, a point made in the Bible where Jesus casts the swine into the sea. But Christianity understood humanity's distinctness from nature as a *gift* from God. 'I have given you all things', says God: 'Every moving thing that liveth shall be meat for you.'

The Enlightenment philosophers increasingly located the source of human distinction in mankind itself, writing excited essays about the innate 'dignity of man' and humanity's capacity for self-development. While fish worshipping corresponded to a feeble control over nature, so this notion of human uniqueness corresponded to a society that was developing science, technology and industry. Our 'dominion' over nature came to be seen not as a gift from God but as the product of our own hands.

Those who argue that human beings and animals are equal, devalue humanity. As animal rights academic Paola Cavalieri notes [in *The Animal Question: Why Nonhuman Animals Deserve Human Rights*, 2001], new notions of animal rights are the result of changing definitions of humans, with a shift from 'high-sounding claims about our rationality and moral capacity' to 'work on a much more accessible level'. The ability to feel pain is the definition of moral worth suggested by Peter Singer (who calls it sentience) and Richard Ryder (who calls it painience). Human beings' superior mental abilities are apparently of no moral consequence: Singer talks about humans' 'self-awareness, and the ability to plan for the future and have meaningful relationships with others', but argues [in *Animal Liberation*] that they are 'not relevant to the question of inflicting pain—since pain is pain'. Here commonality with other human beings (and animals) is based on our central nervous systems. We are all part of a 'community of pain', says Ryder. Singer suggests that a human life is worth (a bit) more than an animal's, because we have a slightly higher level of sentience. We should therefore treat sentient animals as we would a mentally handicapped human being.

Others take a behavioural psychological approach. Primate studies have found that they form relationships among members of the group; that they have some kind of memory of events; that they can use twigs and rocks as tools and have different 'tool cultures' for different groups; that they can communicate with one another and can learn basic signs to communicate with humans. Here the question of moral value is decided in a laboratory or in field tests, weighed on the basis of cognitive and awareness skills. Humans come out better than chimps, but it is a quantitative rather than qualitative difference. . . .

Finally, others take DNA as their measure of moral value. Studies have shown that we share some 98.4 per cent of our DNA with chimpanzees, and an even greater proportion of our genes. When recent research showed that humans shared a closer evolutionary relationship with chimps than previously thought, calls started for chimps to be removed from the *pan* genus and welcomed into *homo*. Many drew the assumption that shared DNA made chimpanzees into moral agents. 'Could a chimp ever be charged with murder?', asked the UK *Daily Mail*. . . .

How Humans Are Different

Human beings are not just a variation on chimps. What is at question is not *awareness* of our world, but *consciousness*. Humans are the only beings that are an object for themselves: that not only exist but know that they exist; that don't just act, but reflect on their activity. 'Man makes himself', is the title of a book on human history by archaeologist V. Gordon Childe. He notes that biological evolution selects characteristics that will be useful for a particular environment—a tough hide for protection, fast running to escape predators, or sharp claws with which to kill. Human beings have virtually no useful biological adaptations: we are slow, naked and thin-skinned. Instead we consciously fashion our own adaptations, from clothes to cars to weapons. Rather than being a product of evolutionary improvement, we improve ourselves.

This is not a question of degree: it is a question of kind. Over time evolution has produced increasingly complex species, which have a greater control over and awareness of their environment—from bacteria to plants to reptiles to primates. Evolution is the equivalent of a plane speeding up on a runway, and then with the emergence of humans it takes off and operates according to completely different laws. Whatever chimps' and gorillas' genetic similarity to humans, they are primarily creatures of evolution. A chimp community from two million years ago would be completely indistinguishable to one today. . . .

Who knows what the key ingredient was that allowed human beings to take off. Some scientists suggest that it was a refinement in the vocal tract, allowing a greater range of sounds for speech. Certainly consciousness is intrinsically social: we only become aware of ourselves as individuals by seeing ourselves in the eyes of others; we only have inner thoughts through the common symbols of language. . . .

In the development of humans, there was a weakening of biological adaptation and an increasing reliance on culture. We became upright, leaving our hands free; our hands lost their adaptations for swinging (chimps) or bounding (gorillas) and became primarily for manipulation of tools; our mouths

The Moral Difference

Human beings are fundamentally different from their animal kin in the wild. They have the capacity to make choices, they possess free will and have the responsibility to act ethically and respect the rights of other human beings. Why? So these others can carry out their morality responsibilities on their own initiative. Human beings, in short, are free and morally responsible.

Tibor R. Machan, "The Myth of Animals Rights,"
lewrockwell.com, July 25, 2000.

lost their adaptations for tearing food (such as tough tongues and lips, heavy jaws, large teeth) and became sensitive and versatile for speech. The hand and the mouth are the key human organs. Aristotle called the hand the 'organ of organs' because of its versatility. Thomas Aquinas looked down on the 'horns and claws' and 'toughness of hide and quantity of hair or feathers' in animals: 'Such things do not suit the nature of man. ... Instead of these, he has reason and hands whereby he can make himself arms and clothes, and other necessities of life, of infinite variety'. Reason, Aquinas said, was 'capable of conceiving of an infinite number of things' so it was fitting that the hand had the 'power of devising for itself an infinite number of instruments'.

Some suggest that we have been in denial about the moral implications of Darwinism for the past 150 years. Richard Ryder argues: 'Thanks to Darwin, many of the huge and self-proclaimed differences between humans and animals were revealed to be no more than arrogant delusions. Surely, if we are all related through evolution we should also be related morally'. In fact, the opposite is true. First, knowledge of Darwinism shows just how much we have managed to break free of the process of natural selection that holds every other living creature in its yoke. Second, in finding that we evolved rather than were created by God, perhaps we truly became our own gods. After all, what kind of species manages to find out the secret of its own origins?

Crossing the Species Barrier

In purely practical terms, modern society is more distinguished from animals than ever before: we live more than ever in conditions of our own creation, immune from natural pressures of hunger and cold. Yet there is a curious dissonance between practical reality and consciousness. Whereas in the past human beings' practical mastery went hand-in-hand with an expanding consciousness, now the two have come apart. While practical mastery continues apace, it lacks the moral foundations to justify it. As a result, we are effectively living in two worlds: one composed of the things we do, and one of the things we can justify. Behind this lies doubt about the point to human existence. E.O. Wilson's 1978 book *On Human Nature* argued: 'We have no particular place to go. The species lacks any goal external to its own biological nature'. Wilson perceptively noted how such 'evolutionary ethics' were a fill-in for 'the seemingly fatal deterioration of the myths of traditional religion and its secular equivalents'. It was a loss of faith in our ability to make our own history that encouraged the view that we are just a bundle of nerves and DNA.

Some humans are now trying to cross the species barrier, seeking again a kinship with animals. Indeed such is the real content of many of the primate experiments with chimps and gorillas. Jane Goodall in Gombe National Park was less observing chimps from outside than trying to become one with them, empathising with their courtships and fights and injuries. . . .

This blurring of the boundaries between animals and humans means a loss of moral sense, and a disgust at humanity.

... We are in a paradoxical situation today, of using our capacity for consciousness and creativity to devalue that consciousness and creativity. Scientists use their ability to analyse DNA to prove that we are little more than chimps. Philosophers use their reasoning powers and the accumulated knowledge of human history to try to prove that humans have no special ethical value. ...

There are severe consequences of holding human life so cheap. For a start, it is demoralising, drumming home the notion that our lives are futile. There are practical implications too. Animal research has produced key medical breakthroughs, from insulin to heart transplants to vaccines. Many of us would now be dead were it not for these discoveries. Now that animal rights concerns hold back research, this will mean needless human deaths in the future. Meanwhile, in wildlife sanctuaries in the developing world the welfare of chimps or tigers is placed above that of local villagers. The biologist Jonathan Marks sums up the crude calculations he heard from a colleague: 'A British professor thinks there are too many Asians and not enough orangutans.'

It is only a human-centred morality that can provide for fertile and equal relationships among human beings. We should relate to each other and respect one another as conscious, rational beings, rather than as DNA databases or collections of nerve endings. Attempts to find equality between humans and animals are founded in a loss of moral compass, and a disgust at humanity. As such, they are antithetical to historic attempts to fight for human equality. Moreover, it is our sense of humans as a common family that means that we can treat those who lack full agency and rationality—such as disabled people and children—with love and respect. These humans live in a network of relationships, and are loved and valued by those around them.

None of this means that we should be nasty to or disinterested in animals. Wanton torture is wrong, though less because of the pain it causes to the animal than because it reflects badly upon the torturer. The same level of animal pain, existing for a clear purpose in a slaughterhouse or a science lab, would be entirely justified. A proper relationship to animals consists in using them in a controlled, conscious manner—for the varied ends of the butcher, the nature photographer, the poet, the scientist, or the pet-owner. These relationships with animals are founded on our different aims and values, and as such are moral. A human-centred approach could mean spending hours in the wild studying animals, or painting and admiring them—but seeing them through a human eye rather than trying to escape our humanity.

What is at question is the position from which we see the world. Taking a bear-centred perspective makes no more sense than a DNA-centred perspective. Humans are the measure of all things: morality starts with us.

> *"It should be no surprise that many in the animal-rights movement use violence to pursue their man-destroying goals."*

Animals Rights Activists Are Terrorists

Alex Epstein

In the following viewpoint, Alex Epstein claims that animal rights activists who resort to violence to thwart animal experimentation are terrorists. Epstein argues that animal experimentation is vital to medicine, and those who would put the interests of animals before the interests of people are dangerous to both science and society. According to Epstein, right-thinking people should make sure that animal rights terrorists are jailed for their crimes and that the antihuman philosophy of animal rights should be condemned. Alex Epstein is a writer for the Ayn Rand Institute, a California-based educational organization advocating rational self-interest, individual rights, and free-market capitalism.

As you read, consider the following questions:

1. What acts of terrorism does Epstein say animal rights activists have used to intimidate those who conduct animal experimentation?

2. According to Epstein, in what way is animal experimentation vital?

3. What is the purpose of rights, as Epstein defines them?

The "animal rights" movement is celebrating its latest victory: an earlier, more painful death for future victims of Alzheimer's, Parkinson's, and Huntington's disease.

Thanks to intimidation by animal rights terrorists, Cambridge University . . . [in England] dropped plans to build a laboratory that would have conducted cutting-edge brain research on primates. According to *The Times* of London, animal-rights groups "had threatened to target the centre with violent protests . . . and Cambridge decided that it could not afford the costs or danger to staff that this would involve."

The university had good reason to be afraid. At a nearby animal-testing company, Huntingdon Life Sciences, "protestors" have for several years attempted to shut down the company by threatening employees and associates, damaging their homes, firebombing their cars, even beating them severely.

Many commentators and medical professionals in Britain have condemned the animal-rights terrorists and their violent tactics. Unfortunately, most have cast the terrorists as "extremists" who take "too far" the allegedly benevolent cause of animal rights. This is a deadly mistake. The terrorists' inhuman tactics are an embodiment of the movement's inhuman cause.

Why Experimentation Is Vital

While most animal-rights activists do not inflict beatings on animal testers, they *do* share the terrorists' goal of ending animal research—including the vital research the Cambridge lab would have conducted.

There is no question that animal research is absolutely necessary for the development of life-saving drugs, medical procedures, and biotech treatments. According to Nobel Laureate Joseph Murray, M.D.: "Animal experimentation has been essential to the development of all cardiac surgery, transplantation surgery, joint replacements, and all vaccinations." Explains former American Medical Association president Daniel Johnson, M.D.: "Animal research—followed by human clinical study—is absolutely necessary to find the causes and cures for so many deadly threats, from AIDS to cancer."

Millions of humans would suffer and die unnecessarily if animal testing were prohibited. Animal rights activists know this, but are unmoved. Chris DeRose, founder of the group Last Chance for Animals, writes: "If the death of one rat cured all diseases, it wouldn't make any difference to me."

An Anti-Human Position

The goal of the animal-rights movement is not to stop sadistic animal torturers; it is *to sacrifice and subjugate man to animals*. This goal is inherent in the very notion of "animal rights." According to People for the Ethical Treatment of Animals, the basic principle of "animal rights" is: "animals are not ours to eat, wear, experiment on, or use for entertainment" —they "deserve consideration of their own best interests regardless of whether they are useful to humans." This is in exact contradiction to the requirements of human survival and progress, which demand that we kill animals when they endanger us, eat them when we need food, run tests on them to fight disease. The death and destruction that would result from any serious attempt to respect "animal rights" would be catastrophic—for humans—a prospect the movement's most consistent members embrace. "We need a drastic decrease in human population if we ever hope to create a just and equitable world for animals," proclaims Freeman Wicklund of Compassionate Action for Animals.

Extreme Tactics by Animal Rights Group

According to [a 2002 Southern Poverty Law Center report], ARL [animal-rights/liberation] terrorists such as ALF [Animal Liberation Front] and SHAC [Stop Huntingdon Animal Cruelty] regularly employ "death threats, fire bombings, and violent assaults" against those they accuse of abusing animals. Some of the cruelest attacks have been mounted by SHAC against executives for Huntingdon Life Sciences, a British drug-testing facility that uses animals to test drugs for safety before they are tested on people. Indeed, the threats and violence became so extreme that Huntingdon fled Britain out of the fear that some of their own were going to be killed. They had good cause. The company's managing director was badly beaten by three masked assailants swinging baseball bats, while another executive was temporarily blinded with a caustic substance sprayed into his eyes.

Wesley J. Smith, "Terrorists, Too: Exposing Animal Rights Terrorism," National Review *online, October 2, 2002. www.nationalreview.com.*

To ascribe rights to animals is to contradict the purpose and justification of rights—to protect the interests of *humans.* Rights are moral principles necessary for men to survive as human beings—to coexist peacefully, to produce and trade, to provide for their own lives, and to pursue their own happiness, all by the guidance of their rational minds. To attribute rights to nonrational, amoral creatures who can neither grasp nor live by them is to turn rights from a tool of human preservation to a tool of human extermination.

It should be no surprise that many in the animal-rights movement use violence to pursue their man-destroying goals. While these terrorists should be condemned and imprisoned, that is not enough. We must wage a principled, intellectual war against the very notion of "animal rights"; we must condemn it as logically false and morally repugnant.

> *"These [animal] activists ... are part of a relatively new, isolated social movement, and therefore more vulnerable to attacks on civil liberties."*

Animals Rights Activists Are Not Terrorists

Will Potter

In the following viewpoint Will Potter, a freelance journalist, claims that animal rights activists are unfairly being labeled as terrorists by the U.S. government. According to Potter, federal authorities are making such claims because the government's War on Terror has failed to nab any real and dangerous terrorists. Thus, in Potter's view, the government is rounding up relatively harmless activists in order to convince the public that the War on Terror is achieving results.

As you read, consider the following questions:

1. As mentioned in the viewpoint, with what crime were the Stop Huntingdon Animal Cruelty (SHAC) activists charged?

2. Why does Potter describe the arrested activists as "canaries in the mine?"

Will Potter, "Animal Rights Arrests," *ZNet*, May 27, 2004. www.zmag.org. Reproduced by permission of the author.

3. In Potter's view, what should all political activists do in response to the arrests of the SHAC members?

The [George W.] Bush administration sent a calculated message to grassroots political activists [in May 2004]: The War on Terrorism has come home.

FBI agents rounded up seven American political activists from across the country Wednesday morning, and the U.S. Attorney's Office in New Jersey held a press conference trumpeting that "terrorists" have been indicted.

That's right: "Terrorists." The activists have been charged with violating the Animal Enterprise Terrorism Act of 1992, which at the time garnered little public attention except from the corporations who lobbied for it. Their crime, according to the indictment, is "conspiring" to shut down Huntingdon Life Sciences [HLS], a company that tests products on animals and has been exposed multiple times for violating animal welfare laws. [Huntingdon is a British company with branches in the United States and other countries.]

The terrorism charges could mean a maximum of three years in prison and a $250,000 fine. The activists also face additional charges of interstate stalking and three counts of conspiracy to engage in interstate stalking: Each count could mean up to five years in prison and a $250,000 fine.

A Sham War on Terrorism

Since September 11, the T-word has been tossed around by law enforcement and politicians with more and more ease. Grassroots environmental and animal activists, and even national organizations like Greenpeace, have been called "eco-terrorists" by the corporations and politicians they oppose. The arrests on Wednesday, though, mark the official opening of a new domestic front in the War on Terrorism.

Bush's War on Terrorism is no longer limited to Al Qaeda or [its leader] Osama Bin Laden. It's not limited to Afghanistan or Iraq (or Syria, or Iran, or whichever country is next). And it's not limited to the animal rights movement, or even the campaign against Huntingdon Life Sciences. The rounding up of activists on Wednesday should set off alarms heard by every social movement in the United States: This "war" is about protecting corporate and political interests under the guise of fighting terrorism.

To use a non-animal rights analogy, these activists are the canaries in the mine. They are part of a relatively new, isolated social movement, and therefore more vulnerable to attacks on civil liberties. But what happens to them now will happen to other movements soon enough.

The activists arrested are part of a group called Stop Huntingdon Animal Cruelty [SHAC], an international organization aimed solely at closing the controversial lab. The group uses home demonstrations, phone and email blockades, and plenty of smart-ass, aggressive rhetoric to pressure companies to cut ties with the lab. It has worked. The lab has been brought near bankruptcy, after international corporations like Marsh Inc. have pulled out their investments.

To most, this is effective—albeit controversial—organizing. According to the indictment, though, it's "terrorism" because the activists aim to cause "physical disruption to the functioning of HLS, an animal enterprise, and intentionally damage and cause the loss of property used by HLS."

That's like saying the Montgomery bus boycott, a catalyst of the civil rights movement, was terrorism because it aimed to "intentionally damage and cause the loss of property" of the bus company.

Everyone Could Be a Terrorist

It seems the biggest act of "terrorism" by the group is a website. Members of the group are outspoken supporters of illegal direct action like civil disobedience, rescuing animals from

Falsely Labeled as Terrorists

On May 26, 2005 at 6 a.m. . . . these seven activists were arrested at gunpoint by FBI, ATF [Bureau of Alcohol, Tobacco, and Firearms], Secret Service and Homeland Security agents. This after over 100 FBI agents and 11 US attorneys spent time tapping phone lines and email accounts, raiding homes and threatening friends and family with grand jury subpoenas. And all of these resources were spent, or rather wasted on these people that did the sinister act of running a website and writing letters to companies that test on animals. Beware!

Megan McGowan,
"Animal Rights Activists Shouldn't Be Labeled As Terrorists!"
Collegiate Times, *October 20, 2005.*

labs, and vandalism. Whenever actions—legal or not—take place against the lab, the group puts it on the website. The activists are not accused of taking part in any of these crimes.

Such news postings are so threatening, apparently, that the indictment doesn't even name the corporations that have been targeted. They are only identified by single letters, like "S. Inc." or "M. Corp."

"Because of the nature of the campaign against these companies, we didn't want to subject them further to the tactics of SHAC," said Michael Drewniak, spokesperson for the U.S. Attorney's Office in New Jersey, in an interview.

Some of the wealthiest corporations on the planet, and the U.S. Attorney's Office must protect them from a bunch of protesters. This is what the War on Terrorism has become: The Bush administration can't find real terrorists abroad, yet it spends law enforcement time and resources protecting corporations from political activists.

The lawsuit is so outlandish that some activists, who asked that they not be identified, said they don't think it is intended to win. Instead, they see it as an important political move in the War on Terror. In a hearing before the U.S. Senate Judiciary Committee just last week, a U.S. Attorney said the Animal Enterprise Terrorism Act needed to go further to successfully be used against Stop Huntingdon Animal Cruelty. If this lawsuit fails, the Justice Department can say, "We told you so."

So, these activists face a double-edged sword. If they lose, they go to prison, and are labeled "terrorists" for the rest of their lives. If they win, it could be fodder for an even harsher political crackdown.

Their only chance is for activists of all social movements— regardless of their political views—to support them, and oppose the assault on basic civil liberties. Otherwise, in Bush's America, we could all be terrorists.

| "Silence does not protect scientists against intimidation."

Animal Researchers Should Not Be Bullied by Animal Rights Terrorists

Fiona Fox

Fiona Fox is the director of the Science Media Centre, a London-based organization that promotes the work of scientists in the British press. In the following viewpoint Fox worries that the intimidation tactics of animal rights extremists are successfully silencing scientists working in the field of animal research. Fox argues that remaining quiet or giving in to extremists' demands will ultimately hurt the research community and perhaps thwart vital work in medical and pharmaceutical science. Only by uniting against the fear, Fox claims, will scientists be able to win the fight against continued harassment.

As you read, consider the following questions:

1. How many animal researchers are members of Fox's Science Media Centre?

2. According to Fox, what was the response of Britain's Research Defence Society to the forced closure of the Darley Oaks Farm, where guinea pigs were raised for animal testing?

3. According to Fox, in what two ways does silence on the part of the scientific community hamper the fight against animal extremists?

In 2001, the New York stock exchange reopened just days after the attacks of 11 September in a symbolic act of defiance against terrorism. How times change. Earlier this month, the same organisation apparently caved in to intimidation from a small group of animal rights extremists over the flotation of Life Sciences Research, the parent company of the UK-based animal research company Huntingdon Life Sciences.

This loss of nerve came hot on the heels of the closure of a UK-based business that bred guinea pigs at Darley Oaks Farm in Staffordshire, which was forced to shut down by a sustained campaign of intimidation. You might be forgiven for thinking that the extremists are winning.

Whether or not they are winning depends, for me, on whether they are managing to silence the scientific community. And that certainly seems to be happening. I work for the Science Media Centre, an independent press office based in London that was set up in 2002 to encourage scientists to speak out on the controversial stories of the day. On issues ranging from genetically modified crops to designer babies and nanotechnology, the centre has been hugely successful in signing up scientists willing to enter the media fray.

But not so for animal research. Getting scientists to speak on this topic has been a dispiriting affair. The number registered on our database is limited to about 20 brave souls. Most scientists and their institutions in the UK, it appears, are allowing themselves to be silenced on the issue of animal testing by the violent activities of a handful of animal rights extremists.

Terrorists Oppose Democratic, Free Discussion

Professor Steve Bloom, head of metabolic medicine at Imperial College London, is among the many UK researchers who have been targeted by extremists. He has had phone calls threatening violence against his children. Prof Bloom is angry that the actions of a few can undermine open public discussion. And he believes extremists are actually impeding improvements to the [animal welfare] law. 'The terrorists are against democracy. They inhibit free discussion. People are afraid to speak out because they know they might become the next target. 'No one can make an informed decision without free and open discussion. But how can you be informed if the people who have the information are threatened or even attacked whenever they speak out?'

Janis Smy, "Can Doctors Safely Talk about Testing?"
Hospital Doctor, October 7, 2004.

The extremists' actions have led many universities, healthcare charities and drug companies to maintain a "no comment" policy on animal testing. One press officer in a university planning to build a new animal facility says that his proposal to invite the local media in at an early stage was met with horror by colleagues, whose instinct was to keep the project quiet. Another leading university that does animal research recently offered the Science Media Centre a venue for press conferences—but only on condition that the topics steered clear of animal testing. And several press officers from other institutions say it is their policy to remove references to animal research from press releases about medical breakthroughs.

Fortunately, there are signs that such attitudes are changing. Simon Festing, director of the UK's Research Defense Society [RDS], which represents medical researchers in the debate on animal testing, points out that 10 years ago almost no scientists ever spoke out on animal research. But on the day the news broke about the closure of Darley Oaks Farm, the RDS released a declaration of support for animal research signed by more than 700 scientists.

More voices are desperately needed. Hundreds of institutions and tens of thousands of scientists conduct animal research that they consider to be crucial to curing human disease, yet refuse to say so publicly. While individually the reasons for their reticence are often compelling and hard to challenge, collectively this must surely amount to one of the most catastrophic collapses of nerve in our society today. The failure is all the more regrettable when you consider that support for animal testing from the public, government and media has never been greater.

What's more, silence does not protect scientists against intimidation. The long-standing campaigns against Darley Oaks Farm, Huntingdon Life Sciences and more recently the University of Oxford's planned new animal facility show that all too clearly. Extremists targeted these organisations despite the silence of the people who work there.

Keeping silent can even make matters worse, attracting accusations of secrecy and allowing activists' unfounded allegations of malpractice to go unanswered. And there is no evidence that speaking out in the media is the spark for intimidation and attacks. My own straw poll of scientists on our database revealed that most of those who spoke out had not been targeted. And many of those who had spoken out, such as Colin Blakemore, a neurosurgeon at the Radcliffe Infirmary in Oxford, started doing so only after becoming targets.

The way forward is clear. If all those scientists who support animal testing started to say so publicly they would drown out the small number of extremists and make it harder for them to pick out individuals from the crowd. My hunch is that extremists, who clearly prefer midnight attacks to open debate, steer clear of those robust enough to take to the airwaves.

Despite the animal rights activists' apparent successes, the battle over animal research is far from over. While government and the police must continue do their bit, and do it better, this alone is unlikely to stop the attacks. The real test will be whether those who perpetrate physical attacks against those who use animals in experiments will succeed in driving animal research abroad. Only if the scientific community is willing to stand up and be counted will the extremists be defeated.

Periodical Bibliography

The following articles have been selected to supplement the diverse views presented in this chapter.

Gary Block   "The Moral Reasoning of Believers in Animal Rights," *Society & Animals*, July 2003.

Jeffrey Brainard   "Undercover Among the Cages," *Chronicle of Higher Education*, March 3, 2006.

Heidi Brown   "Beware of People," *Forbes*, July 26, 2004.

Kerry Capell   "Animal-Rights Activism Turns Rabid," *Business Week*, August 23, 2004.

Gary Francione   "One Right for All," *New Scientist*, October 8, 2005.

Brad Knickerbocker   "Crackdown on Animal-Rights Activists," *Christian Science Monitor*, March 7, 2006.

David Kocieniewski   "Accused of Aiding Animals by Making Prey of People," *New York Times*, March 1, 2006.

Zeeya Merali   "Animal Activists Flee UK Clampdown," *New Scientist*, May 13, 2006.

Iain Murray and   "PETA: Cruel and Unusual," *Human Events*, Ivan Osorio   January 16, 2006.

R. Scott Nolan   "Activists Seek Personhood for Animals," *Journal of the American Veterinary Medical Association*, September 15, 2003.

Scott Smallwood   "Speaking for the Animals, or the Terrorists," *Chronicle of Higher Education*, August 5, 2005.

CHAPTER 2

Is Animal Experimentation Justifiable?

Chapter Preface

Many American high school teenagers attend at least one biology class in which the dissection of a frog, fetal pig, or other small animal is part of the curriculum. Most schools and teacher organizations support the practice of vivisection in the classroom because it gives students a unique opportunity to see the complex inner workings of a living organism. The National Association of Biology Teachers (NABT), for example, states that "no alternative can substitute for the actual experience of dissection or other use of animals." The NABT also "urges teachers to be aware of the limitations of alternatives."

Opponents of dissection in the classroom believe that studying the internal anatomy of dead animals is not essential for learning. The majority of students, these critics assert, will not be pursuing a career in which intensive biological examination is necessary, and those who might choose to become medical practitioners can acquire this knowledge using other tools such as computer models. The New England Anti-Vivisection Society (NEAVS) further contends that compelling hesitant students to participate in dissection can reduce the value of the exercise. "When forced to use animals in ways the student objects to," NEAVS states, "the student is traumatized and invariably learns *less*."

Because more students are voicing their objection to dissection labs on religious grounds or conscientious concerns, many schools across the nation have begun offering alternatives. Computer simulation, multimedia coursework, and other educational tools have been used as substitute learning aids for those who dissent. These options have allowed students to feel more comfortable about their decision to refrain from dissecting animals. The authors in the following chapter discuss the justification for experimenting on animals beyond the classroom setting. These critics and scholars—like their school-age counterparts—have varying opinions on the ethical merits of using animals to advance scientific knowledge.

> "Observing that all species strive to stay alive and then handicapping ourselves deliberately by not trying to understand the biological world would be just plain stupid."

Animal Experimentation Is Ethical

Adrian R. Morrison

Dr. Adrian R. Morrison works in the Laboratory for Study of the Brain in Sleep at the University of Pennsylvania's School of Veterinary Medicine. As an animal researcher, Morrison believes that animal experimentation is both ethical and necessary to medical progress. In the following viewpoint Morrison defends the ethics of his work by explaining that the human race's overriding duty is to keep itself alive. Humans, like all species, are struggling to survive, he maintains, and medical advancement through animal experimentation serves this purpose. He insists, though, that people have an obligation to look after the needs of animals in their care but that this concern does not contradict the use of animals in purposeful experimentation.

Adrian R. Morrison, "Ethical Principles Guiding the Use of Animals in Research," *The American Biology Teacher*, vol. 65, no. 2, February 2003, pp. 105–08. Reproduced by permission of the National Association of Biology Teachers.

As you read, consider the following questions:

1. According to Morrison, how are humans—of all species—uniquely "burdened?"

2. How does Morrison deflate Peter Singer's notion of "speciesism?"

3. How does Morrison counter the argument that animals have rights?

As a biologist ... I recognize that all species are in a struggle for existence. As the most intelligent species on the planet, we would be extremely foolish to deny this fact and not act on behalf of our own families, friends and, ultimately, our own species by not engaging in biomedical research by all means available. Actually, we would be denying a biological imperative: the drive to survive. Clearly, in this instance one must have the long-range view that biomedical research enhances the opportunity for survival. Of course, our brains endow us with the ability to go beyond 'tooth and claw.' Only we can advance our own interests through the medium of science. Should we go through life arrogantly refusing to use our brains in such research because some philosopher has said that to use animals is wrong? Remember, research has also benefited animals by improvements in veterinary care.

Indeed, it would appear that ignorance of, or ignoring, biology has led a small group of philosophers down a foolish path. A conservation writer [Richard Conniff] has quite directly said that they and their followers have "elevated ignorance of the natural world almost to the level of a philosophical principle."

The following famous statement from the animal rights literature, at the very least, ignores the biological imperative of which I spoke earlier: "If that (abandoning animal research) means that there are some things we cannot learn, then so be it. ... We have, then, no basic rights against nature not to be harmed by those natural diseases we are heir to" (Tom Regan, *The Case for Animal Rights*).

Of course, one can create any world one wants with words. A critical question, though, is would one be willing to live in that world? Should one force it on others for the sake of animals? Neither the philosophers nor their followers have taken a principled, public stand announcing that their world will do without the fruits of modern medicine based on animal research. . . .

With these beliefs made explicit, let me now turn to what I call my 'first principles.' I am quite certain the vast majority of scientists would readily subscribe to all five of them.

First Principles

1. Our first obligation is to our fellow humans. I have already addressed this idea from a biological point of view. Observing that all species strive to stay alive and then handicapping ourselves deliberately by not trying to understand the biological world would be just plain stupid. Indeed, I think it is my most powerful argument, one that no philosopher can defeat. But can one also support this choice philosophically? I believe so.

We are a species unique in our cognitive abilities: to use just a few examples, we create beautiful sculptures, write on philosophical issues, and devise just laws. These laws, as well as tradition handed down from long ago, bind us together in a moral community. Yet, we are autonomous beings living in that community. Only we, of all species on Earth, can be held accountable for our deeds, judged guilty in a court of law. We are burdened in a way that no other species is, even to the extent of caring for other species. These responsibilities make us special in my view and warrant special consideration and compassion. I think it follows that we owe it to our fellow man to alleviate the pain and misery of disease through biomedical research.

Furthermore, our capacity to suffer extends far beyond that of any animal. Immediate pain is one thing and something we must always consider when using animals in research. But I think now of mental suffering: the sense of loss of a child to disease or the despair of a teenager condemned to a restricted life due to a spinal cord severed in a head-on collision while playing football. We can empathize directly with these fellow humans. Being more certain of their suffering than that of any animal, we would be remiss in not putting our fellow humans first by doing research that might eventually help someone. To lack such empathy—and various animal-rightists have evidenced such a lack in their public statements—is inhuman and inhumane.

2. *All human beings are persons.* The average person says: of course! But not Peter Singer, author of *Animal Liberation*, called the 'bible' of the animal rights movement. He reasons that parents with a deformed or mentally defective infant, one with Down syndrome, to use one of his examples, would be justified in rejecting (euthanizing) this 'non-person,' for a baby only becomes a person (protected by law) at one month of age. This act would bring them more happiness if they then had a normal infant. Singer comes from the utilitarian wing of the branch of philosophy called ethics. The utilitarian perspective, at least as carried forth by Singer, allows one to seek the greater good or happiness offered by the normal replacement. This approach would be 'convenient' but dangerous, not to mention that many with Down syndrome or other 'defects' can develop into a reasonably productive and apparently happy person.

Singer is very explicit in his views. He states: "Likewise, we cannot justifiably give more protection to the life of a human being than we give to a non-human animal, if the human being clearly ranks lower on any possible scale of relevant characteristics than the animal." Animals with cognitive abilities can be persons in Singer's view. He believes that we should

Moore. © 1998 Universal Press Syndicate. Reproduced by permission.

abandon belief in the sanctity of human life and no longer exclude animals from our moral community. . . .

Singer emphasizes the concept of 'speciesism,' which means
that treating members of other species without considering
their interests just because they are animals is akin to racism.
This concept drives his thinking. Singer says that we should
not treat members of other species differently than we treat
members of our own just because the former are not humans.
Although he states that he wishes to elevate animals, I think

he drags humanity down to the level of animals with an emphasis on the capacity of all creatures to suffer pain. But the human species is so much more than that. We are a social, highly cognitive species with the capacity to participate in the suffering of people thousands of miles away. This enables rescue operations aided by people from far away after an earthquake or flood. Again, this makes us special in my view. Certainly, we should not treat members of another species with wanton cruelty just because they are not human—in this sense we are considering their interests, but our special duty to fellow humans warrants the use of other species in biomedical research.

3. Animals are not little persons. This principle strikes at the heart of the dilemma faced by a scientist who is very fond of animals, enjoys their company, and yet uses them in research. Although we know they are not little persons, we create our pets as such. I have a young cat, Buster, who captured my heart during his kittenhood. If I stopped walking while he was near me, he would lie on my feet so I would pet him before moving on. He would often stand on my chest while I lie in bed and look closely at me while purring very close to my face. What he was thinking, I will never know. . . .

Yet, for most of my career I used members of his species in my research on sleep mechanisms because, due to their size and habits, cats are well suited for neurophysiological studies on sleep and other phenomena. How could I do this? Indeed, I asked myself several times a year whether I really wanted to continue. The answer was always 'yes.' It came down to faith in the process of science and knowledge of medical history, a belief that my work would provide a bit of knowledge ultimately useful for solving a human problem. Otherwise, it could not be justified. Now, our work involves rats, and I am relieved. To one who keeps a rat for a pet, however, this would not be a satisfactory solution, again emphasizing the point that we decide what the animal is to be in relation to us.

4. We have a great obligation to the animals under our control. No words express this principle better than a passage from a book popular when I was a boy. For some reason the following conversation burned itself into my mind. In *My Friend Flicka* by Mary O'Hara, rancher Rob McLaughlin is speaking with one of his sons about a wild mare that had broken loose from their corral with the noose of a lariat around her neck:

> "What if it did choke her?" asked Howard. "You always say she's no use to you." "There's a responsibility we have toward animals," said his father. "We use them. We shut them up, keep their natural food and water from them that means we have to feed and water them. Take their freedom away, rope them, harness them, that means we have to supply a different sort of safety for them. Once I've put a rope on a horse, or taken away its ability to take care of itself, then I've got to take care of it. Do you see that? That noose around her neck is a danger to her, and I put it there, so I have to get it off"

The point is that although laws administered by the Public Health Service and the Department of Agriculture govern the use of animals in the laboratory, animal welfare in the laboratory must begin with the scientist. It is the scientist's competence and knowledge of the literature that determine whether the animal's participation is for a noble cause. The process is not perfect, I admit, but these standards represent an important ideal. . . .

Our obligations we commonly call 'rights': for example, the right to proper food and water when under our care and the right to be treated humanely. Some philosophers emphasize these moral rights. Indeed, they are embodied in law. But these 'rights' are far from saying animals are our moral equals, something the majority of students recognize intuitively, I am sure. They do not approach [animal rights philosopher Tom] Regan's extreme view quoted earlier. For Regan, who comes from the rights branch of ethics, argues that animals have 'inherent value,' which proscribes our harming them. He argues that they are conscious and goal-oriented; therefore they are 'subjects of a life,' the quality that gives them the inherent value upon which we cannot trample. His stance would leave us helpless in the face of nature. . . .

5. Good science requires good animal care, but bureaucracy does not necessarily equate with increased welfare. With governmental regulation comes a certain amount of bureaucracy. One must accept this because many regulations have improved laboratory animal welfare. Thus, scientists must submit a research proposal for review and approval by a committee of scientists, veterinarians and non-scientists before the research may be undertaken. I think the process is a good one, for it ensures that the plan is methodologically sound and that the welfare of the animal subjects is optimized. Required daily oversight of an institution's animals by veterinarians is also good for both the animals and the quality of the experiments.

But animal-rightist pressure has pushed us, or rather, the United States government, beyond these reasonable demands. Thus, under the illusion created by animal rights pressure claiming that scientists are bent on using animals even though there [are] other equally adequate instruments, the U.S. Congress passed legislation stating that a scientist must show that a thorough review of the literature has revealed no alternatives. We do this, even while knowing that our searches will come up empty; for after 40 years in research on a particular subject, who better than that scientist knows the answer? When another way presents itself, the scientist will take it for ethical as well as scientific reasons. . . .

Philosophy Must Apply to the Real World

Scientists are not aloof, cold-blooded individuals working under some set regimen . . . ; ethical considerations accompany their efforts in the laboratory. I accept, though, that one may disagree with my line of thinking, even rejecting the use of animals in research. In doing the latter, however, one must present his or her fellow human beings with a rational substitute, one that will work in the real world. To date, no one has succeeded. The philosophical leaders of the movement, Regan and Singer, have created unnatural worlds with words and then demolished each other's worlds with more words with philosophical jousting, still agreeing on the need to end all animal use—a political end. Their worlds may have relevance in the corridors of a philosophy department, but they have little meaning in rooms of two institutions close to me, The Hospital of the University of Pennsylvania and Children's Hospital of Philadelphia.

> "If we would not want done to ourselves
> what we do to laboratory animals, we
> should not do it to them."

Animal Experimentation Is Unethical

David Thomas

In the following viewpoint David Thomas asserts that because science does not condone experimenting on nonconsenting humans, it cannot ethically condone experimenting on animals, which never can give consent. Furthermore, if the medical community refrains from the former because of the pain such experiments would inflict, then it must logically refrain from the latter. Animals feel pain, Thomas insists, and to experiment upon them against their will is as cruel and unethical as it would be to conduct experiments upon people without consent. David Thomas is a lawyer and chairman of the Royal Society for the Prevention of Cruelty to Animals.

As you read, consider the following questions:

1. What historical examples does Thomas give of experiments involving nonconsenting humans?

David Thomas, "Laboratory Animals and the Art of Empathy," *Journal of Medical Ethics*, vol. 31, April 2005, pp. 197–202. Copyright © 2005 British Medical Association. Reproduced by permission.

2. In what way is the Helsinki Declaration important to Thomas's argument about the ethics of human and animal experimentation?

3. In the author's view, what is the difference between the deontological philosophical approach to human experimentation and the utilitarian philosophical approach to animal experimentation?

It is not clear whether Shylock would have been opposed to animal experiments. But he should have been, if he was being consistent in his ethics. He understood that, when determining how we should treat others, we should put ourselves in their shoes and ask how we would feel in the same circumstances. In other words, we should empathise. Just as Jews suffer in the same way as Christians if they are poisoned, so do animals. Like Christians and Jews, animals bleed if pricked.

In this article I will argue that consistency is the hallmark of a coherent ethical philosophy and that the obvious comparator with animal experiments is non consensual experiments on people. We regard the latter as unethical, so we should the former. As a society we have no difficulty in empathising with the victims of human experiments. Horror at the thought of being experimented upon is no doubt why we regard the practice as abhorrent. It should not take a big leap of imagination to empathise with the victims of animal experiments as well. In short: if we would not want done to ourselves what we do to laboratory animals, we should not do it to them.

Animals Suffer

Crucially for the debate about the morality of animal experiments, non-human animals suffer just as human ones do. [Seventeenth-century philosopher René] Descartes may have described animals as "these mechanical robots [who] could give such a realistic *illusion* of agony" (my emphasis) but no serious scientist today doubts that the manifestation of agony is real, not illusory. Indeed, the whole pro-vivisection case is based on the premise that animals are sufficiently similar to us physiologically, and for some experiments behaviourally too, for valid conclusions to be extrapolated from experimenting on them.

Of course, the nature and degree of suffering will not always be identical. Some species of animal will suffer less than people in eqvvialent situations, and people probably experience greater distress at witnessing someone close to them suffer than many animals would, adding to the totality of suffering in the human context.

Equally, however, lab animals will sometimes suffer more than people would, sometimes physically, sometimes psychologically. Unlike Terry Waite, who composed several novels in his head as a coping mechanism during his five years of captivity, animals are (as far as we know) not fortified by a sense of mission or injustice and do not know that their suffering will eventually come to an end.

The law has sometimes been slow to recognise that animals suffer. However, the European Union now accepts that animals are sentient beings and therefore qualitatively different from other traded "products". The European Patent Convention and th European Patent Directive each acknowledge that the genetic engineering of animals raises moral issues precisely because the engineered animals are liable to suffer; in principle, a patent could be refused on these grounds. And, in the UK, a licence to conduct an experiment on animals is only required if it is liable to cause "pain, suffering, distress or lasting harm". Nearly three million laboratory animals fell within this definition in 2003.

Suffering, indeed, lies at the heart of all morality. We have moral codes precisely because our behaviour may adversely affect others. It is not surprising, therefore, that animal experimentation has become one of the ethical issues of our time.

In a recent survey carried out by MORI [Market & Opinion Research International] for the [British] Coalition for Medical Progress (CMP), over two thirds of respondents said they were either very or fairly concerned about the issue. The Animal Procedures Committee (APC), the government's advisory body, has recently entered the ethical debate in its report on the cost: benefit test which lies at the heart of the Animals (Scientific Procedures) Act 1986. "Cost", of course, refers principally to animal suffering. The APC's contribution is intelligent but flawed in one crucial respect, as I will explain.

The Battle For Hearts and Minds

The CMP is a newly formed coalition of mulitnational pharmaceutical and contract testing companies (such as GlaxoSmithKline (GSK) and Huntingdon Life Sciences (HLS)), provivisection pressure groups such as the Research Defence Society (RDS), bodies funding animal research like the Medical Research Council, and a trade union, Amicus (which has members at HLS). The fact that yet another lobby group has been set up shows how crucial the battle for hearts and minds on this issue has become. It is fair to point out that many CMP members have a large financial interest in animal experiments.

It is beyond dispute that the present government, ever ready to promote British business, has recently entered the propaganda fray firmly on the side of animal researchers. It contributed an astonishing £85 000 towards the cost of the MORI survey. In 2002 the Prime Minister publicly supported Cambridge University's controversial planning application to extend its primate facility. Rather embarassingly for him, his intervention came on the very day that BBC's *Newsnight* carried the British Union for Abolition of Vivisection's exposé of the suffering endured by primates at the university's existing facility.

The Ethical Issue In a Nutshell

So the battle lines are drawn, sometimes literally. Although there are, increasingly, arguments around the scientific efficacy of vivisection, at root it is an ethical issue: is it justifiable to inflict suffering on animals when it is not for their benefit but rather for the benefit of those doing the inflicting (or those they purport to represent)? As with all ethical dilemmas, the proposition is capable of neither proof nor disproof. If a person's political opinions are merely the rationalisation of his or her instinctive response, so it is with matters of ethics. We react to a given situation at an emotional level and then find the reasons to justify our position. The assumptions we make in addressing an issue will often determine the outcome, and those assumptions will often be the product of our cultural conditioning. Vivisection is no different from other issues in this respect.

The 18th century Scottish philosopher David Hume put it like this:

> The approbation of moral qualities most certainly is not deriv'd from reason, or any comparison of ideas; but proceeds entirely from a moral taste, and from certain sentiments of pleasure or disgust, which rise upon contemplation and view of particular qualities or characters.

Adam Smith's view was that the general rules of morality are founded upon experience of what, in particular instances, our moral faculties and sense of propriety approve or disapprove. None of this means, of course, that rational thought has no place when considering ethical issues. As a minimum, we should, firstly, ensure that we have sufficient facts to make a reasonable judgement; and, secondly, strive for consistency across ethically comparable issues. The debate about animal experiements suffers from a deficiency in both these prerequisites, as I will try to explain.

I will focus on those animal experiments which can truely be said to be designed to address particular human diseases.

They are, in fact, a minority of those carried out but it is here that the rival ethical positions are most sharply engaged.

A Secret System

Animal experiments in this country are shrouded in secrecy. Under section 24 of the Animals (Scientific Procedures) Act 1986, the Home Secretary could be sent to prison for up to two years were he to desclose information given to him in confidence by a researcher. The RDS advises researchers to mark everything they send the Home Office "in confidence" to try to prevent disclosure. A few years ago, Smith Kline French (as it then was) took a judicial review all the way to the House of Lords in an attempt to stop the medicines regulator even *referring* to test the data (which SKF had supplied) when considering applications from other companies. Fortunately the attempt failed, but this is the secrecy mentality. Occasionally companies openly admit that they prefer their rivals to conduct "blind alley" research, irrespective of the cost to lab animals.

The Home Office claims that it makes its own judgement about what is confidential, but usually seems to find a reason to join in the conspiracy of silence.

The outcome of some research is published, of course, but only if the researcher finds it advantageous to do so. He or she is unlikely to highlight the animal suffering involved. Negative results are rarely published. As result, duplication is rife, as international institutions and the industry itself now acknowledge. Where results are published, an article in the *BMJ* has recently highlighted the flaws in the system. The authors concluded: "Systematic bias favours products which are made by the company funding the research. Explanations include the selection of an inappropriate comparator to the product being investigated and publication bias."

The public is therefore denied the information on which to make sound ethical judgements about animal experiments.

It has to rely on the media, which traditionally prefers easy sensationalism to painstaking investigation and stories about animal rights militancy to serious argument. Animal protection groups feel they have to conduct undercover investigations to educate the public.

The Ethical Judgement At The Heart of The Legislation

Crucially, the culture of secrecy means that the legislation cannot work properly. The cost: benefit test is a moral judgement. Before he grants a licence for animal experiments, the Home Secretary is enjoined to weigh the likely "adverse effects" on an animal against the likely benefits of an experiment. That is, of course, a value laden judgement. How much suffering (if any) is acceptable? Does it depend on the species? What about the fact that the animal may die in the experiment, or be killed when it is no longer required? Should commercial benefit suffice? Should society just do without certain products, such that we do not need to worry about their safety? What about fundamental research, from which the benefits are by definition speculative?

There is no arithmetical formula to be applied to these ethical questions. In a mature democracy, how they are answered should reflect informed public opinion. But, this is not possible if the public does not really know what is going on and has no opportunity of influencing regulatory decisions, at however general a level. According to the Home Office, most of its inspectors—who in practice run the system—have previously held licences to experiment on animals, and therefore inevitably bring a pro-vivisection ethical perspective to their task.

Many believe that the government should publish detailed information about animal experiments—what they involve for the animals, their purpose, and their results—unless the researchers can, in an individual case, make out a strong objection. That would reflect the presumption of openness contained in the Freedom of Information Act 2000 (FOI Act), which has just come fully into effect. Information can be made public in anonymised form, in order to protect researchers from any risk of attack; information which is truly commercially sensitive can be omitted for as long as it retains such sensitivity.

Only in this way can there be the informed debate essential for formulation of ethical principles. It remains to be seen how much difference the FOI Act will make.

So, the first prerequisite to a reasoned ethical judgement—the availability of sufficient information—is missing with animal experiments. What about consistency across comparable issues?

Most people would accept that an ethical philosophy should be internally consistent, insofar as possible, and that similar cases should be treated alike. Otherwise, the philosophy is likely to be opportunistic and self serving. To paraphrase John Donne: no ethical issue is an island.

In reaching our view about animal experiments, we should therefore search for a valid comparator and test our view about the former against our view of the latter. The obvious—and I believe correct—comparator is non-consensual experiments on people. In both cases, suffering and perhaps death is knowingly caused to the victim, the intended beneficiary is someone else and the victim does not consent.

The APC rightly raises the question of consistency in its discourse on the ethics of vivisection. However, it chooses the wrong comparator. It suggests that the "appropriate point of comparison should perhaps be with an 'improved' food animal industry". Certainly, there is an ethical overlap between the way we treat food animals and the way we treat lab animals. However, the much more pertinent comparator is non-consensual experiments on people and it is surprising that the APC missed it.

Recent Examples of Non-consensual Experiments on People

Recent history has witnessed many examples of non-consensual experiments on people. For example:

- the barbaric experiments carried out by Nazi and Japanese scientists during the second world war;

- the long running syphilis experiments on black people in Alabama over four decades up to the 1970s;

- the radiological experiments conducted at the Burden Neurological Institute in Bristol [England] during the 1950s and 1960s by British scientists for the US Office for Naval Research. According to *The Ecologist*, holes were drilled at random through the skulls and into the brains of the institute's patients. Steel electrodes, which had been coated with a radioactive chemical, were then sent deep into the brain via these holes, and electric shocks pumped through them. Some of the patients later had tumours deliberately induced in their brains.

Sometimes, the human victim gives no consent at all; on other occasions, he or she may give consent but not on an informed basis. In November 2001, BBC Radio 4's *File on Four* carried a damning report on the practice of some pharmaceutical companies, particularly in Eastern Europe and Africa, of abusing the principle of informed consent in clinical trials, including with children and mentally vulnerable people. Animals of course, cannot give any form of consent—informed or otherwise. I will return to the question of consent because it is central to the debate.

Why Experiments on People and on Animals Are Comparable

Some people will argue that, despite the superficial similarities, non-consensual experiments on people and experiments on animals are not ethically comparable. I have described these arguments below.

People have greater value than animals. It is said that, on the one hand, all people have equal intrinsic value and that, on the other, all people have greater value than all (non-human) animals. So, it is concluded, experimenting on people is unethical whereas experimenting on animals is ethical. There are two points here. Firstly, judging relative value is a subjective, wholly unscientific exercise, not least because the criteria one chooses will almost inevitably determine the outcome. There is no set of obviously correct objective criteria ready to be plucked off the shelf. It rather depends who you ask. Just as for each human being our own existence is inevitably the most important, however altruistic we may try to be, to the laboratory rat its existence matters more than anyone else's.

Secondly, and more importantly, why should the fact (if this is what it is) that A has more value than B mean that A is at liberty to cause pain to B for A's benefit? This is the crucial gap in logic which pro-vivisectionists rarely address. Let us accept for the sake of argument that it was provable that the human species was more important than other species—whether because people generally (though not always) have greater capacity for rational thought, may have greater self awareness, are better able to empathise, or have more sophisticated culture. It is not explained why those attributes mean that we can cause pain to those we relegate further down the hierarchy of value. And, if cruel exploitation of *other* species is justified on a relative value basis, then, logically, so must cruel exploitation *within* our species. Some people, indisputably, have greater capacity for rational thought, have greater self awareness, are better able to empathise, or have a deeper cultural appreciation than other people. However, most people do not conclude that the more endowed are for that reason entitled to cause pain to the less endowed for their own benefit.

The racist, the religious fundamentalist, and the misogynist do, of course, discriminate in their treatment of others according to the hierarchies of value they espouse. The majority of people may profoundly disagree with these hierarchies, but we cannot prove *empirically* that they are misconceived. Once one has breached the moral dam by allowing relative value to be the justification for cruel behaviour in one situation (vivisection), there is no rational basis on which one can tell someone that he does not have the right to be cruel to another person he genuinely (if misguidedly) believes to be of lesser value.

The important point is that the Nazis experimented on Jews *because* they regarded them as being of less value; those carrying out syphilis experiments on black men in Alabama no doubt privately justified them on the basis that they were "only" blacks. The US Bill of Rights deemed slaves to be worth only half a person, with the predictable exploitative results. In Honduras, Guatemala, and Brazil they kill street children by the thousand, because, after all, they are "only" street children, of no more value than last night's rubbish.

In truth, relative value is a very dangerous criterion for making ethical judgements.

People are more intelligent than animals. Supporters of vivisection also point out that people are more intelligent than animals. This, it is claimed, is a morally distinguishing feature. It is, of course, true that people are generally more intelligent than animals (at least according to our own perception of intelligence). However, intelligence is a morally neutral attribute, not least because no moral choice is exercised in acquiring it. We do not give greater rights to the Nobel prize winning scientist than to the unemployed labourer. As Jeremy Bentham put it over 200 years ago in his well known epithet (his italics):

> The question is not, Can [animals] *reason*? Nor, Can they *talk*?, but, Can they *suffer*?

In any event, as Bentham noted, some animals are clearly more intelligent than some people. For example, many animals are more intelligent than people with severe learning disabilities or advanced senile dementia. If intelligence were the determining factor, it would be at least as justifiable to experiment on those people as on those animals.

Only people can exercise responsibility. A linked argument is that, in the mantra of New Labour, rights and responsibilities are the flip sides of the same coin. No one is entitled to enjoy rights unless also willing to exercise responsibility. As people can and do exercise responsibility, they should, it is argued, therefore enjoy the right of not being experimented upon; animals, on the other hand, often do not exercise responsibility (in the way we understand that concept) and are therefore entitled to no concomitant right.

In fact, there is no logical reason why one's right to protection from physical harm should be conditional on what one can give back. No sensible person would deny babies, the mentally handicapped, or the comatose protection from harm because they cannot exercise responsibility.

In truth, there is no ethically relevant criterion which differentiates experimenting non-consensually on people from experimenting on animals. Ultimately, all that the proponent of vivisection has to fall back on is the fact that humans belong to one species and other animals belong to other species: "we are human and they are only animals". This is a truism but one only has to state it to see that it has no intrinsic moral relevance. There may be a natural inclination, even a genetic disposition, to "protect one's own", but as Richard Dawkins acknowledged in *The Selfish Gene*, speciesism (the word first coined by Richard Ryder) has "no proper basis in evolutionary biology". Why, then, do we allow it to determine our ethics?

Consent by People

As I have indicated, the question of consent lies at the heart of the debate about experiments on people and experiments on animals. Experiments on people are sometimes permitted by law and supported by accepted norms. Indeed, the *Declaration of Helsinki: Ethical principles for medical research involving human subjects* (the Helsinki Declaration), as amended in October 2000, says that "[m]edical progress is based on research which ultimately must rest in part on experimentation involving human subjects". However, consent is crucial; without it, the experiment may not be carried out. There are three types of situation where consent is relevant in the case of experimental treatment on people:

- *Healthy volunteers.* Healthy individuals—typically students needing money—take part in trials for new drugs for which they have no therapeutic need. Companies such as GSK advertise for volunteers in publications such as the Big Issue. The Helsinki Declaration emphasises the importance of informed consent: "each potential subject must be adequately informed of the aims, methods, sources of funding, any possible conflicts of interest, institutional affiliations of the researcher, the anticipated benefits and potential risks of the study and the discomfort it may entail". Consent can be withdrawn at any time "without reprisal". Similarly, the Nuremberg Code, which arose out of the post-war Nuremberg Trials, says that "[t]he voluntary consent of the human subject is absolutely essential". Again, the basic principle is that consent can be withdrawn.

- *Patients who have capacity.* Patients sometimes consent to treatment which, although experimental, may benefit them. People suffering from AIDS provide the obvious example. The Helsinki Declaration describes this as "medical research combined with medical care". Additional safeguards are put in place. The benefits and risks of the procedure in question must be tested against the best current prophylactic, diagnostic, and therapeutic methods and the patient must be given access to the best treatment identified by the study at its conclusion. Again, informed consent is key. The patient must be told which aspects of his care are related to the research.

- *Patients who do not have capacity.* The Helsinki Declaration provides that "[s]pecial attention is . . . required for those who cannot give . . . consent for themselves". Presumably, experimentation is only permitted where the person without capacity stands to benefit directly from the process. In the UK, the law gives a high level of protection to patients without capacity, even for non experimental treatment. For example, under section 58 of the Mental Health Act 1983 a registered medical practitioner, before embarking on a course of psychiatric treatment for a patient who is incapable of understanding its nature, purpose, and likely effect, must consult two other people who have been professionally concerned with the patient. It must be convincingly shown that the treatment is in the patient's best interests. In some circumstances the consent of the High Court must be obtained before treatment is given to patients lacking capacity. What happens is that, where the safeguards are met, the law in effect presumes that the patient would have given consent had he or she been able to—because the treatment is in his or her best interests.

In each of these cases, consent is either volunteered or presumed; and in each case the subject's interests are paramount.

Animals and Consent

Animals, of course, cannot give consent. In a therapeutic setting, they rely on their owners to give consent on their behalf. The fact that treatment may be experimental is no bar, provided again that the particular animal may benefit. As with patients lacking capacity, the consent of the animal is, in effect, presumed if the treatment is in its best interests.

Animal experiments, by contrast, never benefit the particular animals experimented upon and are not designed to. This is why the correct comparison is with *non-consensual* experiments on people. A devil's advocate might nevertheless argue that, as with people without capacity, a lab animal's consent might sometimes be *presumed*. He might paint an optimistic scenario in which a mouse is adequately fed and watered and is housed in a laboratory in a way that is environmentally enriching and comfortable. He might also ask us to imagine that the procedures to which the particular mouse is subjected are only mild, such as the occasional taking of a blood sample, and not the more invasive procedures to which many lab mice are subjected (such as the creation of cancerous tumours and ascitic monoclonal antibody production).

Of course, the mouse would prefer not to be subjected to any procedure. But a rational mouse in its position, so the argument could run, might conclude that its life in the laboratory is nevertheless better than life outside, where it would have to search for food and live in constant danger from predators. It might judge that the loss of freedom and the occasional mild discomfort (under our scenario) are worth the security gained. Even if it is likely to be killed prematurely, it might reason that, but for its proposed use in an experiment, it would not have been born in the first place. Better to have a life cut short than no life, it might ponder in an insightful moment.

In reality, even our hypothetical mouse might well prefer to take its chances in the wild. It is a reasonable assumption that primates and domesticated species such as dogs and cats would be most unlikely, under any circumstances, to swap freedom in the wild or a comfortable home for life in the laboratory. Clearly, one could not look to researchers (or government inspectors immersed in the culture of lab animal research) to make an impartial judgement that an animal would have given its consent had it been able to. In addition, the suffering experienced by lab animals is usually greater than mild discomfort, often far greater, even ignoring the distress caused by confinement in unnatural conditions.

However, the important point for the purpose of philosophical discourse is that it is *theoretically possible* to conceive of cases where, *looked at from an animal's perspective*, the cost of being involved in an experiment might be outweighed by other considerations, in the same way as a poor student [contemplating volunteering for medical trials] might make that judgement. Crucially, however, prevailing morality treats the two situations very differently. The law is simply not interested in whether an animal might be presumed to consent to an experiment. Its interests are overridden, ultimately rendered at naught. By contrast, the interests of the human experimental subject are always paramount. Intriguingly, the Helsinki Declaration and the Nuremberg Code embody the fundamental difference in approach. The Helsinki Declaration requires that experiments on people must, where appropriate, be based on information derived from animal experiments; and the Nuremberg Code says that the experiment "should be . . . based on the results of animal experiments".

In other words, the codes stress the importance of consent with experiments on people but brush it aside when it comes to experiments on animals. There is a complete absence of consistency. Lord Winston recently fell into the same trap. He complained that doctors trying out new IVF techniques were effectively experimenting, without informed consent, on patients and babies. His solution? More experiments, necessarily without any consent, on apes and other primates.

Benefit to Other Animals

It is often pointed out, in defence of animal experiments, that animals also benefit from them (from the development of veterinary drugs and so forth). So they may, although in fact most experiments on animals for the benefit of animals are in the context of the farming and pet food industries—in other words, for (human) commercial benefit. In any event, here again the glaring inconsistency in approach manifests itself. The proposition is that it is justifiable to experiment on, say, a dog (against its will) so that dogs as a species may benefit. But if that is right, it must, by parity of reasoning, also be justifiable to experiment on a person (against his will) so that people generally will benefit. However, very few pro-vivisectionists subscribe to this view, at least openly.

Experiments on animals and non-consensual experiments on people are obvious comparators because both involve physical and psychological suffering for an unwilling, sentient victim. In each case consent is neither sought nor presumed and the victim is not the intended beneficiary.

However, society treats the two cases very differently. This is because ethical sleight of hand is deployed. Different ethical principles are applied to the two types of experiment.

With non-consensual experiments on people, a *deontological* approach is taken. The prevailing view is that such experiments are *inherently* wrong, whatever the potential benefits to others. Even where consent is given, the interests of the experimental subject are emphasised. The Helsinki Declaration states as one of its key principles: "In medical research on human subjects, considerations related to the well-being of the human subject should take precedence over the interests of science and society". Science engages in a self-denying ordi-

The Nonconsenting Human Guinea Pig

One notable case in human experimentation involved an Irish servant girl, Mary Rafferty, who entered the Good Samaritan Hospital in Cincinnati in 1874, with an ulcerated tumor on the side of her head, caused by a bad burn. Her physicians diagnosed the ulcer on her scalp as cancerous and apparently attempted to treat her condition surgically. When they believed that her situation could not be remedied, they proceeded to experiment on her. One of Mary's physicians was interested in experiments that Dr. David Ferrier had undertaken with dogs using electric shock to determine the localization of epilepsy. The experiments with Mary are described as follows:

> When the needle entered the brain substance, she complained of acute pain in the neck. In order to develop more decided reaction, the strength of the current was increased by drawing out the wooden cylinder one inch. When communication was made with the needles, her countenance exhibited great distress, and she began to cry. Very soon, the left hand was extended as if in the act of taking hold of some object in front of her; the arm presently was agitated with clonic [alternately contracting and relaxing] spasm; her eyes became fixed with pupils widely dilated; her lips were blue, and she frothed at the mouth; her breathing became stertorous [horase and gasping]; she lost consciousness and was violently convulsed on the left side. The convulsion lasted five minutes, and was succeeded by a coma. . . .

This particular example illustrates a persistent pattern in issues of human experimentation: despite her death a few days later and her unnecessary suffering through the experimentation, her death certificate stated that she had died from cancer.

"The Absurdity of Vivisection," ca. 2000.
http://www.vivisection-absurd.org.uk/.

nance: the interest of the individual trumps that of humanity as a whole, *even though* this probably slows the search for a cure for AIDS.

With animals, by contrast, the approach is a kind of *utilitarianism*. The law allows scientists to cause pain to animals if *others* might benefit. The Royal Society [for the Prevention of Cruelty to Animals] has recently argued that it is the alleged benefits of animal experiments which justify them. What it apparently failed to notice is that, if all that was needed for moral justification was a successful outcome, experiments on people would also be justified—indeed, much more so because people are indisputably a much better scientific model than animals for inquiries into human disease.

Some people, of course, do adopt a utilitarian approach to non-consensual experiments on people. The *BMJ*'s correspondent at the Nuremberg trial of Nazi scientists, Kenneth Mellanby, was prepared to justify those experiments which produced benefits. For example, he praised the notorious paper on typhus vaccines which an SS medical officer, Erwin Ding, published in 1943 as an "important and unique piece of medical research" which might lead to 20 000 people being saved for every victim of the research. We have, fortunately, advanced as a society from the Machiavellian ends and means guide to a moral life—except when it comes to animals.

In making the sort of moral judgement discussed in this article, the best guide, as Shylock realised, is to empathise. The *New Oxford Dictionary of English* defines empathy as "the ability to understand and share the feelings of others". The *Oxford English Dictionary* definition is a little more sophisticated: 'the power of projecting one's personality into (and so fully comprehending) the object of contemplation'. As a moral principle empathy finds best expression in St Matthew's Golden Rule: "Do unto others as you would have them do unto you". If I do not want pain inflicted on me, I should not inflict it on others. The reason we should include animals in our circle of compassion, as Albert Schweitzer put it, is because they, too, can suffer.

The ancient Greek poet Bion summarised it in this way: "Boys stone a frog in sport, but the frog dies in earnest". In other words, we should look at things from the perspective of the victim—human or animal—not that of the would-be exploiter. By this yardstick, animal experiments must be immoral, just as non-consensual experiments on people are. In each case, the degree of immorality is in direct proportion to the degree of suffering caused—experiments causing severe suffering are more immoral than those causing only mild, transient suffering.

Consistency demands that, if we condemn one form of highly invasive physical exploitation, we must condemn all forms. In matters of ethics, the identity of the victim—black or white, Aryan or Jew, man or woman, human or non-human animal—should be irrelevant.

| "*Monkey models are vital to evaluate promising new drugs for efficacy.*"

Using Primates in Medical Experimentation Is Justifiable

Scientific Steering Committee of the European Commission

The European Commission works to advance the interests of its twenty-five member nations. The commission's Scientific Steering Committee advises on matters of health and consumer protection within those nations. In the following viewpoint the committee argues that nonhuman primates are valuable to medical research because they most closely resemble humans in terms of genetic structure. Most significantly, chimpanzees, macaques, and rhesus monkeys are useful as test subjects for new vaccines and therapies designed to counter human diseases. Without the use of nonhuman primates in drug trials, the committee maintains, diseases such as hepatitis, malaria, multiple sclerosis, and AIDS may never be eradicated.

As you read, consider the following questions:

1. What is the significance of Council Decision 1999/575/ EC, according to the committee?

Scientific Steering Committee of the European Commission, "The Need for Non-Human Primates in Biomedical Research," *Statement of the Scientific Steering Committee of the European Commission*, April 4–5, 2002, pp. 1–4. Copyright © 2002 European Communities. Reproduced by permission.

2. What does the committee believe are the two compelling reasons to use nonhuman primates in biomedical research?

3. What animals were used in clinical trials to prove the effectiveness of the Hepatitis C vaccine?

For finding new ways of improving the living standards of humans and animals the scientists use a lot of different approaches. Some of them do not involve live animals, including *in vitro* [outside a living body] techniques, modelling and epidemiological studies. However experiments on live animals are powerful ways of better understanding the complex biological mechanisms. The community is very aware of the consequences of those experiments on the living conditions of the animals involved in experiments. As a consequence a whole set of regulations have been published to avoid unnecessary suffering during the experiments and to provide optimum living conditions during their whole lives (in particular D86/609/EEC, Council Decision 1999/575/EC).

In the Council Decision 1999/575/EC, it is stated that " . . . , accepting nevertheless that man in his quest for knowledge, health and safety has a need to use animals where there is a reasonable expectation that the result will be to extend knowledge or to be the overall benefit of man or animal, just as he uses them for food, clothing and as beasts of burden". The question remains however to weight the costs on the experimental animals and the benefits for the future of humans or animals.

That type of questions is particularly sensitive when primates are involved in experiments. The reasons for this are said to be related to their high cognitive abilities and complex social life which are more easily disrupted than those of other animals by living conditions in laboratories and more specifically during the experiments.

Why Primates Are Needed

The Scientific Steering Committee (SSC) believes that there are scientific reasons why primates will be particularly useful in future European research programs. It should allow the scientific European community to contribute better to the future of human health. It should also insure that the experiments are done under good laboratory practice. By contrast, the SSC however does not feel competent to decide whether or not to use primates in research but that it should be better commissioned by the European Group of Ethics of Sciences and New Technologies of the European Commission. If it is accepted that the use of primates in research is ethical, those animals should be housed and treated in a way that fulfils their species-specific requirements and avoids any unnecessary suffering. . . .

The Scientific Steering Committee considers that non-human primates are required in biomedical research for the following reasons:

1. To ensure safety. Many new vaccines or biologicals must be assessed for specificity and safety in a "near-human" immune system before they enter the clinic.

2. To determine the efficacy of non-human primate models for infections for which no other suitable animal models exist. These so-called "proof of principle" studies are critical in catalysing interest and development capital for development and clinical trials.

It is important to note that to develop specific vaccines, non-human primate models are often required because of safety risks and the chance of unexpected autoimmune or hyper immune reactions and even enhanced infection and or disease (e.g. Respiratory Syncitial Virus). This problem becomes clear when one examines the very specific interactions that parasites and viruses have with their hosts. For instance they are often able to evade the immune system by mimicking immune molecules or altering the regulation of these immune molecules. In most cases their interactions with their host are so species specific that they can only be studied *in vivo* [within living bodies] in hosts very closely related to man.

The following 5 examples, which are far from being exhaustive, illustrate the above:

1. *AIDS*: The epidemic is still rapidly spreading and, with more than 40 million infected, a vaccine is desperately needed. The etiologic agent HIV-1 is an example of a virus with a very complex interaction with the immune system and a very limited host range. It only readily infects humans and to a lesser extent chimpanzees. Macaques are an important surrogate model which when infected with SIVsm [simian immunodeficiency virus, Sooty Mangabey strain] develop an AIDS-like disease which is almost indistinguishable from AIDS in humans. . . .

2. *Malaria*: This is a major cause of human morbidity and mortality in developing countries that is having more impact on developed countries each year. In sub-Saharan Africa up to 2 million children under 5 years of age die from malaria annually. The relationship between the parasite and the host is quite specific, such that human malaria parasites will not infect rodents. They do however infect some non-human primate species, and other malaria parasites of non-human primates are very closely related to the human parasites. Therefore, using both old world and new world monkey models, the relationship between the parasite and the host can be investigated to identify therapeutic and prophylactic possibilities. Although considerable research can be done *in vitro*, the parasite has obligatory intra-hepatic developmental phases that are not amenable to *in vitro* cultivation. To date primates have been used as pre-clinical screens for a variety of new vaccine candidates. . . . Dif-

ferent malaria vaccines will require different immune responses . . . and well-characterised models with similar immune responses to humans (such as macaques) are essential in vaccine development. New malaria drugs will have to work effectively *in vivo*, and many drugs that are effective *in vitro* fail *in vivo*. Monkey models are vital to evaluate promising new drugs for efficacy. More recently genetically modified parasites of primates have been developed and the modifications are allowing vital insight into the critical areas of interaction between the parasite and the host.

3. *Tuberculosis*: One third of the world's population is estimated to be infected with TB. It is a major killer in its own right, and combination with HIV is proving even more of a problem. The current vaccine, BCG, is highly variable in efficacy (in some trials it is ineffective) and existing drugs require long-term treatment and suffer from problems of increasing resistance. Highly virulent new strains such as the Beijing strain are now spreading within Europe, with potentially serious results. Mouse and guinea pig models are used to screen potential new vaccines and drugs, however their patterns of disease and their immune responses are often markedly different from those seen in humans. Recently a careful analysis of two macaque models . . . has shown the value of these two models and their similarity to the human situation. These models are now being used to screen and select among new candidate vaccines before embarking on the complex, protracted and expensive clinical phase.

4. *Hepatitis*: Hepatitis C is the major cause of chronic liver disease leading to hepatocellular carcinoma in humans. More than 200 million people are infected with this virus throughout the world and most of them are unknowing carriers. Hepatitis C cannot be cultured [*in*

vitro] and the only other species other than man that can be infected is the chimpanzee. Early HCV vaccine studies in chimpanzees have begun to show progress but non-human primate research is essential to bring a truly effective vaccine to the clinic. Thanks to studies in chimpanzees which are still alive and healthy today, millions of doses of a very successful Hepatitis B vaccine have been given World-wide. However, Hepatitis B is still transmitted and many new infections occur daily. New less expensive HBV vaccines are required for developing countries to halt and eliminate this chronic human pathogen.

5. *Immune-based diseases*: Non-human primate models of immune-based clinical disorders, such as rheumatoid arthritis, multiple sclerosis, type I diabetes, allergy/asthma and transplant rejection, are needed for the development and evaluation of new immunomodulatory/immunosuppressive therapies. This is in particular the case with biological reagents that by their species specificity work insufficiently in rodent models and of which the potential toxicity in humans is insufficiently clear to test them directly in patients.

There is an increasing need of non-human primates as models for CNS [central nervous system] biology and disease. Multiple sclerosis is one such disease for which there is no cure. MS is an invalidating neurological disease with an underlying autoimmune etiology affecting one in 1,000 young adults. ... The close genetic, immunological and virological relation with humans makes non-human primates an excellent model of this disease.

Why Alternatives Fail

Thus the problems faced in developing vaccines or therapeutics against these modern day plagues can be summarised as follows;

Recent Medical Advances Achieved Through Primate Research

1980s

- Processing of visual information by the brain.
- Treatment of congenital cataracts and "lazy eye" in children.
- First animal model for research on Parkinson's Disease, enabling doctors to more accurately research human Parkinson's Disease.
- Heart and lung transplant to treat cardiopulmonary hypertension.
- First Hepatitis B vaccine.
- Rhesus monkey model for AIDS used to establish the effectiveness of early administration of AZT in cases of diagnosed infection.

1990s

- Lead toxicity studies help U.S. fight childhood lead exposure.
- First controlled study to reveal that even moderate levels of alcohol are dangerous in pregnancy.
- Parent to child lung transplants for cystic fibrosis.
- Monkey model developed for curing diabetes.
- Naturally regenerative mechanism discovered in the mature primate brain, spurring new research toward curing Alzheimer's [Disease and] other degenerative brain disorders.
- Rhesus and cynomolgus monkey kidneys developed for use in diagnosing influenza.
- Development of anthrax vaccine.

2000s

- Monkey model developed to study the effects of malaria in pregnant women and their offspring.
- Dietary restriction without malnutrition provides major health benefits and may extend maximum lifespan.
- Rhesus monkeys are now prime model for development of HIV treatments and potential vaccines. There are 14 licensed anti-viral drugs for treatment of human immunodeficiency virus (HIV) infection alone.

California Biomedical Research Association,
"Fact Sheet: Primates in Biomedical Research." ca-biomed.org.

Host-viral/parasite relationship:

1. For instance some agents such as HCV and malaria intra-hepatic stages cannot be cultured *in vitro* or, they are so species specific that they only infect humans or other closely related primates.

2. An infectious agent may only cause disease due to its specific interaction with the affected host. A good example is HIV-1 which causes disease in almost all humans, but very rarely in chimpanzees.

Specificity of new generation drugs/biologicals:

1. New generation therapeutics are often so specific that sometimes a change in a single amino acid can result in the difference between a beneficial or deleterious effect. These positive or negative effects cannot be predicted by computer models nor by testing in rodents. Often these important side effects can only be detected in specific primate models.

2. Outbredness and the need to consider genetic resistance & susceptibility:

3. Inbred species of mice and even transgenics cannot predict accurately for how long a drug, biological, or vaccine will work or possibly cause adverse effects in an outbred population. An outbred population with specific characteristics, which resemble the human population, is often the most relevant model. Unfortunately, the numbers of captive bred animals needed to maintain this "outbred quality" are high. Smaller colonies of non-human primates will result in a smaller genetic pool in which the predictable value will be lost, or may even result in selective inbreeding, defeating one of the most important needs of primates for research. Thus large, diverse, well-characterised, captive-breeding colonies are needed in Europe to maintain this outbred character.

> *"Can there be any compelling ethical defence of using creatures so like ourselves in ways that we would find unbearable?"*

Using Primates in Medical Experimentation Is Unjustifiable

John Gray

John Gray argues in the following viewpoint that it is unethical to use nonhuman primates in medical experiments. According to Gray, scientists use apes in experiments because they are close to humans in their mental capacity and genetic composition. Gray suggests, however, it is precisely these near-human characteristics that should persuade primate researchers to abandon their work. In Gray's opinion, experimenting on apes is tantamount to experimenting on humans. John Gray is a professor of European Thought at the London School of Economics and the author of Straw Dogs: Thoughts on Humans and Other Animals.

As you read, consider the following questions:

1. To Gray, why is the issue of "consent" immaterial to the arguments for or against primate experimentation?

John Gray, "The Best Hope for Animal Liberation Is That Humans Kill Each Other in Wars," *New Statesman*, vol. 133, no. 4674, February 9, 2004, pp. 29–31. Copyright © 2004 New Statesman, Ltd. Reproduced by permission.

2. How does Gray deflate secular humanist views that place humans in a superior position to the animal kingdom?

3. According to the author, what is the "chief difference" between animals and humans that allows humans to believe they have dominion over other species?

In [Franz] Kafka's story "A Report to an Academy", an ape called Red Peter delivers a lecture to a learned society in which he gives an account of the life he led before he acquired human ways. Captured on the Gold Coast (now Ghana), Red Peter was transported in a cage to Hamburg [Germany]. In that city, he reports, he faced two alternatives—the zoological gardens or the variety stage. Life in the zoological gardens meant only another cage, so he chose the stage. It was not easy to get into the variety hall, but once there Red Peter was an enormous success. Soon he learnt to talk like a human, and it was not long before he achieved what he termed "the cultural level of an average European". His stage performances enabled him to enjoy a distinctly human way of life. As he described it in his report to the academy: "When I come home late at night from banquets, from scientific receptions, from social gatherings, there sits waiting for me a half-trained little chimpanzee, and I take comfort from her as apes do."

Kafka's story is cited in J.M. Coetzee's *The Lives of Animals*, a profound fictional meditation on the contradictions that beset our attitudes to other animal species. The story of Red Peter is a fantastical version of the fate that befell many apes, and—as one of Coetzee's characters notes—there were real-life prototypes of Red Peter. In 1912, the Prussian Academy established a research centre on the island of Tenerife to study the mental powers of apes; and in 1917, the director of the centre, Wolfgang Köhler, published some of the results of this in his celebrated study *The Mentality of Apes*. Like Red Peter, Köhler's apes underwent a period of training designed to induce them to adopt human ways. Among the pedagogic methods used was slow starvation, with the apes being repeatedly shown and denied food until they developed something resembling human faculties.

It is not clear how researchers today would assess the results of this experiment, but Köhler—one of the founders of cognitive psychology—seems to have seen it as a success, noting with satisfaction how the captive chimpanzees ran in a circle round their compound, some draped in old strips of cloth and others carrying pieces of rubbish, "for all the world like a military band".

So Like Ourselves

Köhler's experiments were cruel and demeaning to the animals on which they were inflicted, but they are chiefly notable for the deep confusion they exhibit in his—and our—view of our closest evolutionary kin. We have come to view apes as proto-humans, yet we subject them to treatment we would not dream of inflicting on members of our own species. If apes were not similar to us in important respects, many of the experiments to which they are subjected would be impossible or pointless. Few now deny that apes share much of our intellectual and emotional inheritance. They have many of our own capacities and vulnerabilities: they can think and plan, and they feel fear and love. Without these similarities, Köhler's experiments would have been unfeasible and could not have yielded the knowledge he was seeking. Yet these very similarities undercut the ethical basis of such experimentation.

We do not put humans into captivity and starve them in order to test their intellectual abilities because we know that such treatment would cause severe suffering. How can we justify such experimentation on apes, knowing that it can work only to the extent that their capacities—including the capacity to suffer—are much like our own? Can there be any compelling ethical defence of using creatures so like ourselves in ways that we would find unbearable? Or is the answer that the animals used in such experiments are simply unfortunate—that we have them in our power and their suffering is a regrettable but unavoidable result of our using them for our benefit?

The last of these options appears to have been taken by a recent spokesman for Cambridge University. Responding to protests against plans to establish a primate research centre there, he observed that it is an unfortunate fact that only primates have brains like our own. The implication is that it is precisely because apes have many of the capacities of humans that they are used for experimentation. It is true that experimenting on primates is a productive research technique; but if their similarities with us justify using apes in this way, it would surely be even more effective to use humans. The argument for experimenting on primates leads inexorably to the conclusion that it is permissible—in fact, preferable—to experiment on humans.

The Capacity for Suffering

Quite rightly, the idea that humans should be used in painful or dangerous medical experiments evokes intense moral horror; but this has not always been so. Powerless and marginal people—in prisons and mental hospitals, for example—have in the past often been used as guinea-pigs, and it is all too easy to imagine the forcible use of humans in scientific research practised on a far wider scale. The Nazis saw nothing wrong in subjecting members of what they considered to be inferior populations to the most horrible experiments; and there can be little doubt that had the outcome of the Second World War been different, the use of humans for scientific research would have been institutionalised across Europe. No doubt it would have been condemned by a dedicated few, but the historical experience of occupied Europe suggests that the majority of the population would have accepted the practice.

It will be objected that there is a vital difference between using animals for scientific research and using humans: humans have the capacity for consent, whereas animals do not. It is true that adult humans can express their wishes to other humans in ways that even our closest animal kin cannot; but consent is not the heart of the matter. Even if they agreed, it would be morally intolerable to use prison inmates in dangerous medical experiments. No form of consent they might give could make the injury done to them less real; it would only reflect their powerlessness. Similarly, it is not the inability of human infants to give their consent that justifies an absolute ban on experimenting on them. It is the terrible damage we would inflict on them merely to produce benefits for ourselves.

The same is true of experiments on animals. It is not the capacity for consent that is most relevant, but the capacity for suffering. I am no Utilitarian[1], but [utilitarian philosoper] Jeremy Bentham hit the spot when he wrote of animals that the crucial question is not "Can they speak?" Rather, it is "Can they suffer?"

At this point, those who support animal experimentation have a habit of wheeling out some extremely familiar arguments. Animals lack the capacity for personal autonomy, they tell us, and so cannot recognise duties to others. For the same reason, they cannot have rights. Humans have the power of choice, and this entitles them to a moral status denied to other animal species.

The Opposing View

We hear this tired refrain whenever the subject of animals is discussed, but it is significant not so much for any intellectual content it may have, but for what it shows about the lingering influence of religious belief. If you are a Christian, it makes perfect sense to think of humans as standing in a dif-

---

1. One who believes that the best course of action is the one that causes "the greatest happiness for the greatest number."

Results from Primate Research Cannot Be Extrapolated to Humans

Primates have been very disappointing with regard to their ability to predict dangerous side effects of medications, especially pertaining to the induction of birth defects. Aspirin produces birth defects in primates, but not in babies. Almost all currently used medications cause birth defects in some animal species. PCP, better known as angel dust, sedates chimpanzees but causes humans to have severe experiences including paranoia. Nitrobenzene is toxic to humans but not monkeys. Isoprenaline (isoproterenol) doses were worked out on animals, but proved too high for humans. People died as a result. Even when the researchers knew what to look for they were unable to reproduce this effect in monkeys. . . .

What about infectious diseases? Are we able to draw results from primates about viruses? Chimpanzees harbour Hepatitis B asymptomatically. Humans die from it. Vaccines for polio and rabies were tested safe in primates but killed humans. Even the inventor of the polio vaccine, Dr. Sabin, stated under oath that the polio vaccine was long delayed because of misleading results in primates. AIDS researchers have fared no better. The huge number of differences between the immune system of humans and nonhuman primates invalidates any experimental results. Dr. Mark Feinberg, a leading HIV/AIDS researcher stated: 'What good does it do you to test something [a vaccine] in a monkey? You find five or six years from now that it works in the monkey, and then you test it in humans and you realise that humans behave totally differently from monkeys, so you've wasted five years'. Monkeys do not die of AIDS—but humans do.

Ray Greek, "The Absurdity of Primate Experimentation,"
Absurdity of Vivisection Web site, n.d.,
http://vivisection-absurb.org.uk.

ferent category from other animals. Humans have free will and an immortal soul, and these attributes confer an incomparable importance on human life. No doubt we should refrain from cruelty to other creatures, but they have no claim to value in their own right; they are instruments for achieving human ends. Humans have dominion over animals because humans alone are made in the image of God.

Secular thinkers find it extremely difficult to come up with reasons for thinking that the human species has some kind of unique standing in the world. Darwin showed that we share a common lineage with other animals, and subsequent genetic research has shown the closeness of these evolutionary links. Insofar as humans do have morally relevant attributes that other animals lack, it is right to treat them differently. But within a purely secular perspective there can be no good reason for thinking the human species is supremely valuable.

In the context of their beliefs about animals, as in many other areas, secular humanists parrot a Christian hymn of human uniqueness. They prattle on about the supreme value of human personality as if it were a self-evident truth. Yet it is not accepted in most of the world's religions, and is strikingly absent in some—such as Buddhism—that have never thought of other species as mere instruments of human purposes. Secular humanists are adopting the anthropocentric viewpoint of Christianity—while abandoning the theistic belief-system from which it sprang, and without which it is meaningless.

Humans Are the Chief Threat to Animal Welfare

Once Christianity and humanism have been set aside, it becomes clear that the chief difference between humans and other animals is simply that humans have acquired enormous power. In evolutionary terms, the human species has been an astonishing success. In the space of a few thousand years, it has achieved a seeming mastery over its environment, which is reflected in a vast increase in human population. At the same time, humans have had a huge—and almost entirely harmful—impact on other animal species. The mass extinction of wildlife we are seeing throughout the world comes from the destruction of habitat—itself largely a result of rising human numbers. The damage done to the welfare of other animal species by human expansion is on an incomparably larger scale than anything that is done in scientific laboratories. This does not mean vivisection is unimportant—after all, no one thinks that since millions of people are slaughtered in wars it does not matter if some die as a result of murder—but it does mean that anyone who focuses on animal experimentation is missing the big picture.

The chief threat to animal welfare today comes from the unchecked expansion of homo rapiens. Wherever humans have entered a new environment the result has been a wave of extinctions. . . . The history of human relations with other species is a record of almost unbroken rapacity. Wrecking the environment seems to be in the nature of the beast. . . .

One way or another, human expansion will be curbed; and a plausible scenario is that this will occur as a by-product of war. Globalisation supports the present high levels of human population, but its logic is to intensify the struggle for scarce natural resources. Resource wars, such as the two Gulf wars, look set to dominate the coming century. Such conflicts would be damaging to animals as well as humans, but because of their disruptive effect on the global supply chain, their impact on humans is likely to be much more severe. The end result could be a less crowded world in which other species have room to breathe. Homo rapiens is a ferociously destructive creature, but its capacity for self-destruction is even greater. The human behaviour that Wolfgang Köhler was so pleased to observe being parodied by his captive apes may yet prove to be the ultimate guarantee of animal liberation.

> "*[Deadlock] has arisen ... because the animal research community holds an ethical view that the animal movement rejects.*"

The Animal Experimentation Debate Has Reached a Moral Deadlock

Peter Singer

Peter Singer is a professor of bioethics at Princeton University and the author of the influential animal rights book, In Defense of Animals. *In the following viewpoint Singer claims that the debate over animal experimentation has reached an impasse. According to Singer, those who experiment on animals are unlikely to change their view that sacrificing animals is worthwhile to further science. On the other hand, the ethical arguments of animal rights activists are being undermined by violence from extremists within the movement. Although Singer supposes that the extremists' actions may be the result of continual failure to stop animal experimentation, the violence has further divided the opposing camps and reinforced the notion that the debate is deadlocked.*

As you read, consider the following questions:

1. According to Singer, how does the biblical view of the animal kingdom conflict with the naturalist view of Charles Darwin?

2. Why does Singer argue that nonviolent demonstration serves the animal rights movement's cause better than violent actions?

3. In the author's opinion, who bears the responsibility for ending the violence that has become part of the animal experimentation debate?

The debate over animal experimentation appears to be moving rapidly towards a state of mutual incomprehension and deadlock. The [British] home secretary is debating whether to allow the American animal rights activist Dr Jerry Vlasak into Britain after it was reported that he had said that killing five to 15 vivisectors could save millions of non human lives. (He has subsequently denied that he was encouraging anyone to act in this way.) Animal activists have damaged trucks and other equipment used by construction companies working on Oxford University's new animal laboratory. Even this paper [the *Guardian*], in an editorial, likened British animal activists to al-Qaida terrorists.

The outcome of this process is unlikely to be positive for either side. For those who favour experiments on animals, it will mean keeping a low profile and meeting increased security costs. For the overwhelmingly non-violent animal movement, consisting of many millions of people around the world, there is a risk of serious damage from being identified with the handful of activists who are prepared to go beyond peaceful protest.

Conflicting Ethical Views

This situation has arisen, in part, because the animal research community holds an ethical view that the animal movement rejects. That view is, in essence, that animals are things for us to use, as long as we spare them unnecessary pain. The animal activists, on the other hand, reject the assumption that animals are inferior beings, and that their interests should always be subordinate to our own. They see this as "speciesism" —a prejudice against beings that are not members of our own species, and similar in many respects to racist or sexist prejudices against beings who are not members of a dominant race or sex.

Ironically, in this situation, it is the defenders of scientific research who are most likely to cling to an ethic that clearly has an unscientific basis. If we believe the account of creation given in Genesis, including its divine grant of dominion over all animals, then it makes sense to think that we are justified in using animals for our own purposes, as scientists wish to do. But if, on the other hand, we think [naturalist Charles] Darwin was right, and we are all here because of an unplanned process of evolution, there is no reason to assume that human interests should always take precedence over the interests of non-human animals. As [utilitarian philosopher] Jeremy Bentham wrote almost 200 years ago: "The question is not 'Can they reason?', nor, 'Can they talk?', but 'Can they suffer?'"

It may be possible to carry out some experiments on animals that do not cause them to suffer. And it may even be that, consistently with Bentham's principles, one can imagine situations in which, without treating the interests of animals as less weighty than those of humans, the benefits of an experiment on an animal would outweigh the costs to the animal. But the entire institution of animal research, as it exists in Britain today, is based on a different foundation: that animals count for less, and those that we are not especially fond of count for less still. Otherwise, why would Oxford University have said, in defending its proposed laboratory, that "98% of the animals involved would be rodents". Does the university believe that the interests of rats do not count?

Violence Undermines Ethics

Those who oppose treating animals as if they were mere tools for research therefore have a strong ethical argument. But when a few people use violence and intimidation to achieve the desired goal, they undermine the animal movement's ethical basis. In a democratic society, change should come about through education and persuasion, not intimidation.

Those who advocate violence may claim, with some justice, that the democratic process has been tried, and has failed. Despite decades of widespread popular support for reform, little has changed. Even the recent *Guardian* leader that began with the incendiary comparison between al-Qaida and animal rights extremists observed that more should be invested in finding alternatives—and it pointed out that a House of Lords committee stacked with scientists made the same recommendation two years ago. Yet in comparison to the funds that go into research using animals, the amount spent on developing alternatives is still very small. The extremist tactics we are now seeing may well be the result of the frustration caused by the failure of the democratic process to lead even to measures on which virtually everyone agrees.

Nevertheless, I cannot support the use of violence in the cause of animal liberation. It sets a dangerous precedent—or, one might say, it follows dangerous precedents. In the United States, "pro-life" extremists have fire-bombed abortion clinics and murdered doctors who terminate pregnancies. I consider these defenders of the sanctity of human life from conception to be misguided; but no doubt they are just as sincere in their convictions as defenders of animals. It is difficult to find democratic principles that would allow one group to use intimidation and violence, and deny the same methods to the other.

Non-violent responses to the frustrations of the democratic process do less damage to the fabric of civil society. Gandhi and Martin Luther King have shown that civil disobe-

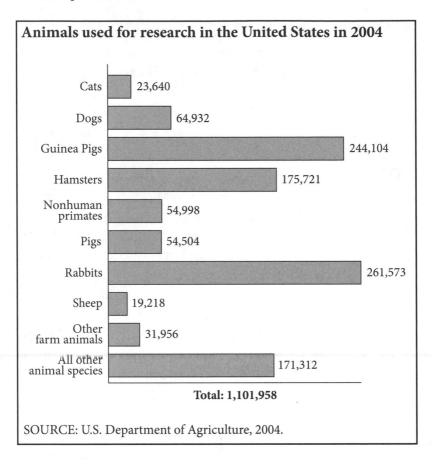

Animals used for research in the United States in 2004

Cats — 23,640
Dogs — 64,932
Guinea Pigs — 244,104
Hamsters — 175,721
Nonhuman primates — 54,998
Pigs — 54,504
Rabbits — 261,573
Sheep — 19,218
Other farm animals — 31,956
All other animal species — 171,312

Total: 1,101,958

SOURCE: U.S. Department of Agriculture, 2004.

dience can be an effective means of demonstrating one's sincerity and commitment to a just cause, while at the same time eschewing violence. Those who break the law openly, and are prepared to pay the price for doing so, are more likely to gain the respect and support of the public than those who strike secretly in the dark, and use fear, rather than persuasion, to change behaviour.

The Scientific Community Must Make the Next Move

Is there a way out of the present deadlock? Some opponents of experiments on animals will be satisfied with nothing less than the immediate and total abolition of all animal research.

In a society that continues to eat meat, however, that is an unrealistic goal. If people think that their enjoyment of the taste of animal flesh is sufficient reason to confine millions of animals in horrific factory farms, transport them to slaughterhouses and then kill them, why would they reject the use of relatively smaller numbers of animals in experiments designed to find cures for major diseases?

The mainstream animal movement has repeatedly condemned the use of violence against sentient beings, human or non-human. My own statements against it now stretch back nearly 20 years. But every large movement attracts extremists who are impatient at the slow pace of change. There is little more that the non-violent majority of the animal movement can do. The next step is really up to the government and the research community. If animal activists could see that serious efforts were being made to find new ways of doing research without animals, the violent fringe of the movement would become even more isolated than it now is.

> "It is possible to achieve fair agreements
> between reasonable people who accept
> that they must give some ground in or-
> der to achieve a peaceful solution."

The Moral Deadlock
Concerning Animal
Experimentation Can
Be Broken

Patrick Bateson

*Sir Patrick Bateson is a professor of ethology at the University of
Cambridge in England. He is also president of the Zoological Society of London's Animal Welfare Committee. In the following
viewpoint Bateson acknowledges that minority extremists' views
on both sides of the animal experimentation debate are unyield-
ing and unlikely to change. He believes, however, that the majority of researchers and animal rights activists may come to an
understanding about continuing some animal research if specific
rules were enacted. According to Bateson, these rules would permit animal experiments if the research was of high value and
the suffering of the animals involved was tolerable. Only by bal-
ancing the quality of the research with its benefit to humans and*

Patrick Bateson, "Using Animals in Research: There Is, Perhaps, No More Contentious
Area of Psychology Than Research with Animals," *Psychology Review*, vol. 11, no. 3,
February 2005, pp. 2–6. Copyright © Philip Allan Updates. Reproduced by permission.

its impact on the animal subjects can all parties, in Bateson's view, resolve the explicit moral dilemma.

As you read, consider the following questions:

1. How does Bateson liken his "shoe shopping" example to the moral debate surrounding animal experimentation?

2. In Bateson's view, under what conditions should animal suffering be tolerated in scientific experiments?

Public concern about animal welfare has increased greatly in recent years. Scientists who simply want to be left alone to get on with their work cannot and should not ignore such concern about the ways animals are treated in laboratories. Nor should they brush aside the animal suffering that can undoubtedly arise in research.

As this conflict intensifies, reason seems to have flown out of the window. The positions on the use of animals in scientific work have become so polarised that useful dialogue between experimenters and their critics is exceedingly difficult. Indeed, animal rights activists have inflicted major defeats on the scientific community. The decision by Cambridge University not to go ahead with a primate facility is one such case.

The Argument for Animal Rights

Although people feel uneasy about the use of animals in research for many reasons, one stream of thought in particular has fed into the strongly held view that animals must not be used in research under any circumstances. Certain morally based actions are absolutely good or bad and should not be influenced by cost-benefit calculations.

It is argued that animals have rights that are as important as those of humans. But what is an 'animal'? Does a rat have the same moral status as a chimpanzee? Does an ant have the same status as a rat? Does an amoeba have the same status as an ant? The answer given by Tom Regan, the most influential philosopher guiding animal rights activists, is that rights should be granted to animals which have beliefs, desires, perceptions, memories, a sense of the future, feelings of pleasure and pain accompanying a rich emotional life, an ability to initiate action in pursuit of desires and goals and a psychological identity over time. Even so, identifying the animals that might qualify for rights on this basis is not easy.

More fundamentally, human rights are part of an implicit contract with the social community; people accept conventions upon which the smooth functioning of society depends and these lead inevitably to the need to honour commitments. In short, rights bring with them responsibilities. These considerations suggest that giving a right to an animal is about as sensible as giving it a vote.

Although the rights position underpinning the wish to stop all research using animals is readily criticised, nobody can doubt the strength with which it is held. The end justifies the means and, for some, that involves intimidation and violence. Laboratories are wrecked, scientists' homes are attacked and their children are abused. But strength of feeling does not necessarily mean that the animal rights activists occupy the moral high ground. Strong ethical arguments are also mounted for the use of animals in scientific studies. In the past, many biologists took the view that they had a right to pursue knowledge for its own sake and this aspect of academic life, highly valued in universities, trumped all other considerations. Not many would adopt such an unvarnished view these days, but most scientists would continue to argue that great benefits flow from biological research. These benefits might be improvements in medical or veterinary practice achieved in the short to medium term or fundamental contributions to the understanding of biological processes. The provision of such benefits is seen as good and morally important.

Critics respond by questioning the motives of biologists, suggesting that the real goals are fame, career advancement

and occasionally fortune, coupled with extraordinary wicked-
ness when it comes to the treatment of animals used in research. An unwillingness to use alternatives to living animals
is attributed to vanity, laziness or conservatism. I would argue
that these are cheap shots. Doubtless some scientists have the
base motives attributed to them. You will find some who are
just as vain, lazy and conservative as some members of any
other group of people. However, in a serious moral argument
it is discreditable to question the sincerity and integrity of
those who hold a different position from yourself. Those who
dislike the use of animals in research are confronted by moral
convictions that are as strongly held as their own.

A more serious moral argument is that animals which suffer in the course of scientific research do not benefit from any
advances in knowledge derived from their suffering. In human
and veterinary medicine, causing pain or suffering in a patient
is considered unethical unless it is for the direct benefit of
that patient. The great majority of us who work on animals in
the course of our research are strongly bound to an ethic of
caring for them. That means that we are forced into accepting
that one moral principle is in direct conflict with another. The
dilemmas seem inescapable. Before considering how they
might be resolved, I shall discuss briefly whether scientists are
correct in their belief that work on animals has led to major
medical and veterinary benefits.

The Value of Animal Research

In justifying the demand that current research be stopped, activists suggest that behavioural work is scientifically trivial, of
no medical importance, could be done without using animals
or would be better done on humans. Most scientists would
disagree and . . . a House of Lords Select Committee, after
hearing both sides, concluded that the case for research on
animals was strong. They also argued that more effort should
be made to find replacements—a view I support.

However, in behavioural biology, necessarily involving work on intact systems, the opportunities for replacements are limited. Even computer simulations of complex systems have to be carried out alongside work on real animals in order to be effective. Studies of animal behaviour should flourish in the interests of both human and, indeed, animal welfare. An understanding of the social conditions necessary for the normal development of behaviour in animals has proved to be of direct medical benefit to humans. For instance, losing a mother early in life can lead to long-lasting mental and physical disorders in humans. Thanks to the work on animals, the developmental processes that depend on interaction with the mother are being uncovered. Effective forms of therapy for humans have been found and brought into practice.

Knowledge of the natural behaviour of animals and the way they respond to stress is improving conditions for farm animals and for those kept in zoos and laboratories. Veterinary practice is powerfully supplemented by behavioural expertise when assessing the condition of an animal or when designing quarters in which the animals should live. An animal's behaviour is one of the best guides to its state of well-being. Training veterinary surgeons to detect abnormalities of behaviour can provide them with quick, non-invasive methods for assessing distress. The knowledge acquired during training is increasingly recognised within the veterinary profession as an important contribution to animal welfare.

As far as the public is concerned, the studies of animal behaviour made famous through television programmes give pleasure and understanding to millions of people. At a practical level, this knowledge of the relationship between the behaviour of animals and their natural environment is of major value when planning the conservation of wildlife. Finally, solving how and why animals behave as they do raises some of the most challenging and exciting problems in science. It is not possible to crack these problems with tissue culture or by computer simulations. . . .

Reconciling Different Moral Positions

Even when people holding utterly different moral positions are totally inflexible and seem set for a fight to the finish, it is possible to devise practical ways of helping the majority resolve the undoubted moral conflicts. The alternative to absolutism on either side of the debate is to respect both positions and attempt to minimise suffering inflicted on animals used in research, while maximising the scientific and medical gains. I believe it is possible to achieve fair agreements between reasonable people who accept that they must give some ground in order to achieve a peaceful solution. . . .

Seemingly irreconcilable views can sometimes be brought together because a lot of one desirable outcome does not have to mean a little of another. It is possible to reconcile a strong moral commitment to understand biology and benefit from such understanding by using scientific methods with an equally strong moral desire to minimise animal suffering. Alternatives can be found to the destructive opposition between the morality of advancing our understanding of the natural world through science and the morality of eliminating the suffering that science sometimes brings with it.

Making Difficult Decisions

Most people consciously, or more often unconsciously, take many different things into account when making everyday decisions. Suppose, for instance, you want to buy a new pair of shoes. You will want good quality and you may well want shoes that are fashionable. At the same time, you are also likely to want to pay as little as possible. You will probably set an upper limit for how much you are prepared to pay and a lower limit for the quality. If you are forced to pay more, you will expect higher quality. I think the analogy is relevant to the present case: a much lower amount of animal suffering would be tolerated in scientific research if the work were not regarded as being important.

A Zoology Professor Expresses His View on Limiting Animal Experimentation

I . . . believe that some work using laboratory animals should continue because there is important work that we should try to do for medical and other reasons. But I also believe that many medical and other biological scientists are not seriously attempting to address the Three Rs [the principles of Reduction (reducing numbers of animals used), Refinement (refining experiments to cause minimal suffering), and Replacement (replacing animal experiments with viable alternatives)] in their work: because they have done a particular type of experiment for several years they see no reason to alter or abandon a 'proven' procedure.

Statements such as 'there is no alternative to using animals for this type of work' are easy to make and difficult to either challenge or sustain with sound evidence. Too many physiologists and other researchers are simply not prepared to step back and ask themselves if they really should be doing so many experiments using live animals.

Malcom Edmunds, "Animals in Research,"
Biologist, vol. 52, no. 5, October 2005.

When I first suggested it at a scientific meeting some 25 years ago, the shoe-shopping analogy grated on many people because they felt that no animal suffering could be justified merely in the name of good science. If the words 'medical benefit' were added to 'good science', the answer seemed clear to most of these critics. Great human suffering—and plenty of it exists in the world—is felt to be worse than the possibility of mild discomfort inflicted on an animal in the course of research. Of course, the likely benefits of biological science for human and animal welfare are not easily predicted. The best bet in general is to back science that is likely to lead to the discovery of fundamental and unifying principles. Many governmental and charitable funding bodies accept that the funding of high quality biological research is one of the best ways of contributing to the medicine of the future. Nonetheless, the delivery of real benefits to humans or animals is uncertain. It was for this reason that I included in the decision rules the probability of generating medically important results. . . .

Decision Rules for Animal Research

For the purposes of making a judgment, three separate dimensions are to be considered:

- the scientific quality of the research

- the probability of human benefit

- the likelihood of animal suffering

Animal suffering should be tolerated only when both re search quality and certainty of benefit are high. Moreover, certain levels of animal suffering would generally be unacceptable, regardless of the quality of the research or its probable benefit. The decision rules used would permit research of high quality involving little or no animal suffering, even if the work had no obvious potential benefit to humans. This feature takes note of the concern of scientists who want to understand phenomena that have no immediate or obvious benefit for humans. . . .

Assessing Quality. Assessing the quality of research presents its own problems. Nevertheless, virtually all funding of future scientific research depends on making informed judgments about how particular projects will develop. Nobody denies that funding decisions are difficult and can be mistaken, but nobody who lives in the real world supposes research funding should be decided by tossing a coin. Similarly, difficult though it may seem, committees judging planned medical research are asked to assess the probability of a therapeutic outcome.

Assessing Animal Suffering. How do we assess suffering? This question is more likely to be asked by members of the scientific community than by many animal rights activists, who seem to think that the answer is obvious. The intrinsic difficulty is that suffering is a subjective state and no person can be sure that another would, in the same circumstances, suffer as they do. The usual way of dodging this ancient philosophical catch is to rely on the similarities between people. So if I suffer when I am burnt, I assume that you, too, will suffer in much the same way when you are burnt. Undoubtedly this is the implicit assumption of most vets when dealing with the issue of pain in animals. If the animal has the same neural equipment for detecting damage and processing the information in its central nervous system as humans and if it behaves in situations that humans would find painful in much the same way as a human, the intuitive rule is that the animal should be treated humanely. Identical arguments are mounted for other aspects of suffering by those concerned about animal welfare. . . .

The assessment of suffering is not straightforward, but can be greatly assisted by expert knowledge. In general, I believe that we can reach a reasonable consensus on what would constitute low, intermediate and high levels of suffering in a particular animal.

Out of the Deadlock

One advantage of a set of rules . . . is the acknowledgment that, in deciding whether a particular activity should be tolerated in a civilized society, more than one thing matters. Both the extreme animal rights activists and my more conservative scientific colleagues tend to suppose that the values they hold dear are the only ones that could possibly be important. Even when people holding such different moral positions are so inflexible and seem set for a fight to the finish, it is possible to devise practical ways of resolving the conflict.

Periodical Bibliography

The following articles have been selected to supplement the diverse views presented in this chapter.

Colin Blakemore	"Medical Experimentation," *Chronicle of Higher Education*, December 2, 2005.
Malcolm Edmunds	"Animals in Research," *Biologist*, October 2005.
Simon Festing	"The Animal Research Debate," *Political Quarterly*, October–December 2005.
Alan M. Goldberg and Thomas Hartung	"Protecting More than Animals," *Scientific American*, January 2006.
Sharon Howe	"Animal Testing Is Both Cruel and Unnecessary," *Independent* (London, England), March 6, 2006.
Roman Kolar	"Animal Experimentation," *Science & Engineering Ethics*, January 2006.
Lancet	"Animal Research in the Post-Genome Era," March 17, 2001.
Edwin H. McConkey and Ajit Varki	"Thoughts on the Future of Great Ape Research," *Science*, September 2, 2005.
Doug Moss	"He Ain't Hairy, He's My Brother," *E: The Environmental Magazine*, March–April 2003.
Nutrition Health Review: The Consumer's Medical Journal	"Is Animal Experimentation Worthwhile?" 2003.
Gina Solomon	"The Lesser Evil," *Earth Island Journal*, Autumn 2002.
Peter Tatchell	"Why Animal Research Is Bad Science," *New Statesman*, August 9, 2004.

CHAPTER 3

Does Animal
Experimentation Aid
Medical Progress?

Chapter Preface

More than 17 million animals are used in medical research in the United States each year. Of these, more than 95 percent are mice, rats, or other rodents. The remainder of animals range from cats and dogs to pigs and sheep to squids and apes. Each animal species is selected because researchers believe it serves as an exceptional model of some aspect of human physiology. As the North Carolina Association for Biomedical Research claims:

> Crayfish are used to study muscle functions. Armadillos are used to study leprosy. Pigs are used to study influenza and to develop new surgical techniques. Woodchucks infected with a virus similar to the human hepatitis B virus are ideal models to study new treatments for the disease. Sheep, because they share anatomic similarities with humans, are becoming popular models to study diseases and injuries of the bones, joints, and muscles. The squid, octopus and sea snail are important models for neurobiological studies.

> Proponents of animal experimentation attest that even the vast array of mice are invaluable to medical research. Some of these rodents are genetically modified so that they can better simulate human biological systems. This has allegedly given researchers a better understanding of Parkinson's disease, cancer, heart conditions, and muscular dystrophy.

The majority of the animals used in research are bred in captivity for this purpose. Their care and treatment is dictated by the Animal Welfare Act (AWA). This piece of legislation, passed in 1966, allows oversight committees to inspect animal research facilities to make sure that the animals in their care are housed, cleaned, and fed properly. It also stresses that pain and suffering must be minimized during procedures. Infractions of the law can result in steep fines or even the closure of the lab in question. The AWA, however, does not delineate what procedures can or cannot be done to animals during experiments.

In the following chapter, some authors debate the appropriateness of animal experimentation in medical science. Defenders of animal research insist that the aforementioned studies have yielded valuable insight into human and animal diseases. Critics, however, maintain that few if any major medical breakthroughs have come about as a result of animal research. Other authors in this chapter address the similar controversy over animals used in drug and toxicity trials.

| "Research using animals has led to some of the most important medical discoveries in history."

Animal Experimentation Is Vital to Medical Research

American Physiological Society

The American Physiological Society (APS) is a national, nonprofit organization devoted to fostering education, scientific research, and dissemination of information in the physiological sciences. In the following viewpoint the APS argues that animals are vital to medical research. According to the APS, animals are living models that can help researchers study the progress and consequences of both human and animal diseases. Animal models also aid in testing drugs before trials with human subjects. Without animal experimentation, the APS maintains, it would be impossible to improve the quality of life for both people and animals.

As you read, consider the following questions:

1. The APS cites three animal biological systems that are similar to those in humans. What are they?

American Physiological Society, "Laboratory Animals' Contributions to Medicine," American Physiological Society, n.d. www.the-aps.org. Reproduced by permission.

2. According to the APS, what animals are aiding in new research on epilepsy?

3. What are three of the ways in which animal experimentation is aiding in veterinary research?

Research in physiology provides the scientific basis for much of medical practice, and is thus critical for maintaining health as well as for the diagnosis, prevention, and treatment of health problems. In order to understand and treat disease, physiologists need to understand how the body works under both normal and abnormal conditions before they can develop ways to prevent and treat disease.

Since some health problems involve processes that can only be studied in a living organism, it is necessary to perform research on animals when it is impractical or unethical to use humans. Additionally, research using animals has led to some of the most important medical discoveries in history. Animal research continues to help humans, as well as animals, live longer and healthier lives.

What Humans Have in Common with Animals

Animal research has helped scientists to understand and find ways to prevent and treat diseases historically (in diseases that are no longer widespread, like polio) and at present (for health conditions that are still prevalent), including:

- Heart disease

- Diabetes and obesity

- Neurological diseases such as Alzheimer's and Parkinson's

- Cancer

- Infectious diseases including AIDS and tuberculosis

- Inflammatory bowel diseases like Crohn's disease

In these and other instances, animals make good research subjects because they are biologically similar to humans. For example, the immune system of mice, the cardiovascular system of dogs, and the reproductive system of guinea pigs all function in much the same way as in humans. Humans also share many of their genes not only with other primates, but also with animals as far removed as mice and fruit flies.

So Why Use Animals for Research?

- Animals are used for biomedical research because it would be wrong to deliberately expose human beings to health risks in order to observe the course of a disease or use humans in invasive experiments to study normal organ function.

- Animals are susceptible to the development of many of the same health problems as humans.

- Their shorter life cycles make it easier to study them throughout their whole life span or across several generations.

- Scientists can better control variables (such as diet, age, weight, and physical activity), which would be difficult to do with human patients.

- Scientists can also change an animal's genes to study genetic diseases that cause illness in people.

Animal research is helping to elucidate the following human conditions:

Obesity and Diabetes: People with obesity and diabetes are at risk for a number of potentially serious complications that can cause premature death. For instance, researchers have used genetically engineered mice to better understand how liver damage occurs in people with Type 2 diabetes.

Epilepsy: People that are born with brain malformations sometimes have a kind of epilepsy that is not easily treat-

Humans Are Equally Vital to Medical Research

'The' use of one rodent and one non-rodent species will predict seven of ten toxic reactions in human beings. About 350 human diseases have an animal counterpart. For each drug tried in humans, about 350 animals will have been tested. Human trials need 3000–4000 participants. They enter studies for no known efficacy benefit to themselves, that being the purpose of the trial to discover. To argue that human beings do not subject themselves to research, research that can lead to harm or even death, is to grievously misunderstand medical science.

Lancet, *"Animal Research Is a Source of Human Compassion, Not Shame,"* vol. 364, no. 9437, September 4, 2004.

able with medicines. Using rats that exhibit the same kind of symptoms, scientists at Stanford University Medical Center were able to study the differences in how the brain functions in rats with epilepsy compared to healthy rats.

Parkinson's Disease (PD): Researchers studying the development of PD have used a mouse model to study genetic changes that occur in brain cells (neurons) during the earliest stages of disease, even before the substantial loss of neurons associated with the classic symptoms of PD occurs. These types of studies could lead to early detection and treatment that would ultimately minimize the severity of symptoms associated with PD.

How Animals Help Us Find Cures

Animals also play a critical role in development of new drugs and new medical procedures to treat diseases. For example, studies in animals were used to establish the safety of drugs that are widely used to treat high cholesterol, ulcers, depression and a slew of other common conditions and illnesses. In fact, almost every drug used in humans is first tested in animals.

Animal studies are done first to give medical researchers a better idea of what benefits and complications they are likely to see in humans. If the new therapy seems promising, it is tested in animals to see whether it appears to be safe and effective. Researchers use animal testing to discover what toxic side effects a drug might have, what doses are safe, and how a drug is absorbed and broken down in the body. Only after scientists have seen that the drug can be safely and effectively used in two or more species of animals do they begin testing in humans.

Scientists sometimes discover such drugs and procedures using alternative research methods that do not involve animals. While there is currently no substitute for animal testing in drug development, scientists are continually looking for other ways to test therapies for safety and efficacy.

How Animals Help Other Animals

Often times, animal research elucidates cures and treatments for ailments that afflict animals and humans alike. Many of these advances can then be used in veterinary medicine to improve the length and quality of animals' lives.

Veterinary medicine has benefited from discoveries found through animal research that alleviates animal pain and sickness and prevents disease in our pets, food animals and wildlife. Just some of the areas where animal research has helped other animals include:

- Development and testing of animal vaccines

- Detection and prevention of infectious diseases

- Food animal health and safety

- Treatments for lameness and arthritic pain

- Development of artificial joints

- Cancer therapies

- Treatment of genetic and acquired heart problems

- Animal responses to exercise

How Animal Research Is Regulated

An important part of doing animal research is making sure that laboratory animals are always treated humanely. The Animal Welfare Act is a law that regulates the use of many animals including dogs, cats and primates in scientific research and drug testing. In addition, the US Public Health Service Act requires that all research institutions receiving federal funds review and approve all research projects using vertebrate animals, and adhere to the guidelines in the "Guide for the Care and Use of Laboratory Animals."

Scientists care very much about the health and welfare of their laboratory animals. In addition to having to follow the rules put in place by their employers and the government, scientists know that unhealthy animals do not yield reliable experimental results.

Animal research is vital to advancing medicine. Physiologists will continue to learn from animals through humane research, with the goal of improving human and animal health and longevity.

| "Many ... important medical advances have been delayed because of misleading information derived from animal models."

Animal Experimentation Is Not Vital to Medical Research

Christopher Anderegg et al.

Christopher Anderegg and his colleagues who wrote the following viewpoint argue that animal research has had little consequence upon human medicine. According to the authors, using animals as models for human physiology has resulted in misleading data and unforeseen consequences in drug testing. The inherent differences between animals and humans have also delayed the proper understanding of how certain diseases progress through human bodies. Instead of investing in more animal research, the authors suggest, science should focus on more clinical research involving people. Christopher Anderegg and his colleagues are members of the Medical Research Modernization Committee, a national health advocacy group that evaluates the benefits and risks of medical research methods and technologies.

As you read, consider the following questions:

1. Why are animal models not useful in predicting psychological problems in humans, according to the Medical Research Modernization Committee report?

2. According to Anderegg and his colleagues, what—at best—can animal testing suggest to researchers? Why do the authors believe such results do not merit continuing animal experimentation?

3. Despite animal testing, what percent of drugs were taken off the market between 1975 and 1999 because of unforeseen health risks?

Proponents of animal experimentation (tests, experiments, and "educational" exercises involving harm to animals) claim that it has played a crucial role in virtually all medical advances. However, several medical historians argue that key discoveries in such areas as heart disease, cancer, immunology, anesthesia, and psychiatry were in fact achieved through clinical research, observation of patients, and human autopsy.

Human data has historically been interpreted in light of laboratory data derived from nonhuman animals. This has resulted in unfortunate medical consequences. For instance, by 1963 prospective and retrospective studies of human patients had already shown a strong correlation between cigarette smoking and lung cancer. In contrast, almost all experimental efforts to produce lung cancer in animals had failed. As a result, Clarence Little, a leading cancer animal researcher, wrote, "The failure of many investigators to induce experimental cancers, except in a handful of cases, during fifty years of trying, casts serious doubt on the validity of the cigarette-lung cancer theory." Because the human and animal data failed to agree, this researcher and others distrusted the more reliable human data. As a result, health warnings were delayed for years, while thousands of people died of lung cancer.

By the early 1940s, human clinical investigation strongly indicated that asbestos caused cancer. However, animal studies repeatedly failed to demonstrate this, and proper workplace precautions were not instituted in the U.S. until decades later. Similarly, human population studies have shown a clear risk from exposure to low-level ionizing radiation from diagnostic X-rays and nuclear wastes, but contradictory animal studies have stalled proper warnings and regulations. Likewise, while the connection between alcohol consumption and cirrhosis is indisputable in humans, repeated efforts to produce cirrhosis by excessive alcohol ingestion have failed in all nonhuman animals except baboons, and even the baboon data is inconsistent.

Many other important medical advances have been delayed because of misleading information derived from animal models. The animal model of polio, for example, resulted in a misunderstanding of the mechanism of infection. Studies on monkeys falsely indicated that polio virus was transmitted via a respiratory, rather than a digestive route. This erroneous assumption resulted in misdirected preventive measures and delayed the development of tissue culture methodologies critical to the discovery of a vaccine. While monkey cell cultures were later used for vaccine production, it was research with human cell cultures which first showed that poliovirus could be cultivated on non-neural tissue. . . .

Nevertheless, society continues to support animal experimentation, primarily because many people believe that animal experimentation has been vital for most medical advances. However, few question whether such research has been necessary or even, on balance, helpful in medical progress.

Contemporary Animal Experimentation

Cancer: In 1971 the National Cancer Act initiated a "War on Cancer" that many sponsors predicted would cure cancer by 1976. Instead, this multibillion dollar research program has proven to be a failure. . . .

Why hasn't progress against cancer been commensurate with the effort (and money) invested? One explanation is the unwarranted preoccupation with animal research. Crucial genetic, molecular, immunologic, and cellular differences between humans and other animals have prevented animal models from serving as effective means by which to seek a cancer cure. Mice are most commonly used, even though the industry's own *Lab Animal* magazine admits: "Mice are actually poor models of the majority of human cancers." Leading cancer researcher Robert Weinberg has commented: "The preclinical [animal] models of human cancer, in large part, stink. . . . Hundreds of millions of dollars are being wasted every year by drug companies using these models." According to Clinton Leaf, a cancer survivor himself: "If you want to understand where the War on Cancer has gone wrong, the mouse is a pretty good place to start."

AIDS: Despite extensive use, animal models have not contributed significantly to AIDS research. While mice, rabbits, and monkeys born with severe combined immunodeficiency can be infected with HIV, none develops the human AIDS syndrome. Of over 150 chimpanzees infected with HIV since 1984, only one allegedly developed symptoms resembling those of AIDS. Even AIDS researchers acknowledge that chimpanzees, as members of an endangered species who rarely develop an AIDS-like syndrome, are unlikely to prove useful as animal models for understanding the mechanism of infection or means of treatment. . . .

Psychology and Substance Abuse: Animal "models" of psychology, traditionally employing painful stimuli to study behavior, have been strongly criticized in part because human psychological problems reflect familial, social, and cultural factors that cannot be modeled in nonhumans. Indeed, most psychologists disapprove of psychological animal experiments that cause animal suffering.

Harry Harlow's "maternal deprivation" experiments involved separating infant monkeys from their mothers at birth and rearing them in total isolation or with "surrogate" mothers made of wire and cloth. Their terror and subsequent psychopathology, Harlow claimed, demonstrated the importance of maternal contact. However, this had been shown conclusively in human studies.

Despite its conceptual shallowness, numerous maternal deprivation studies continue, claiming relevance to human developmental psychology, psychopathology, and even immune and hormone function.

Animal models of alcohol and other drug addiction are similarly ill-conceived, failing to reflect crucial social, hereditary and spiritual factors. . . .

Genetic Diseases: Scientists have located the genetic defects of many inherited diseases, including cystic fibrosis and familial breast cancer. Trying to "model" these diseases in animals, researchers widely use animals—mostly mice—with spontaneous or laboratory-induced genetic defects. However, genetic diseases reflect interactions between the defective gene and other genes and the environment. Consequently, nearly all such models have failed to reproduce the essential features of the analogous human conditions. For example, transgenic mice carrying the same defective gene as people with cystic fibrosis do not show the pancreatic blockages or lung infections that plague humans with the disease, because mice and humans have different metabolic pathways.

Toxicity Testing: Numerous standard animal toxicity tests have been widely criticized by clinicians and toxicologists. The lethal dose 50 (LD50), which determines how much of a drug, chemical, or household product is needed to kill 50% of a group of test animals, requires 60 to 100 animals (usually rats and mice), most of whom endure great suffering. Because of difficulties extrapolating the results to humans, the test is highly unreliable. Also, since such variables as an animal's age,

Animal Models Prove Useless to the Testing of AIDS Drugs

Some of the most successful [AIDS] drugs, the protease inhibitors, were developed when the structure of an important HIV enzyme was discovered by non-animal test-tube methods. One of the first protease inhibitor drugs was indinavir (Crixivan), which progressed to clinical trials on the basis of its anti-HIV activity in test-tube studies using proteins and human cells (but not animal models of AIDS). Tests were done in rats, dogs and monkeys to see how indinavir was absorbed, metabolised and excreted by the body. Ironically, these tests revealed significant differences between the three species. For example, the amount of indinavir absorbed was 14% in monkeys, 23% in rats and 72% in dogs, and rates of metabolism varied too. Until human volunteer studies of indinavir were conducted, the equivalent values for humans were unknown. In fact livers of monkeys generate a unique metabolite of indinavir not seen at all in humans.

British Union for the Abolition of Vivisection (BUAV),
Medical Research: HIV Research Fact Sheet, BUAV Web site,
n.d. www.buav.org.

sex, weight, and strain can have a substantial effect on the results, laboratories often obtain widely disparate data with the same test substances. . . .

Scientific Limitations of Animal Models

Animal studies can neither confirm nor refute hypotheses about human physiology or pathology; human clinical investigation is the only way such hypotheses can be tested. At best, animal experiments can suggest new hypotheses that might be relevant to humans. However, there are countless other, often superior, ways to derive new hypotheses.

How valuable is animal experimentation? The Medical Research Modernization Committee's review of ten randomly chosen animal models of human diseases did not reveal any important contributions to human health. Although the artificially induced conditions in animals were given names analogous to the human diseases they were intended to simulate, they differed substantially from their human "counterparts" in both cause and clinical course. . . .

In contrast to human clinical investigation, animal experimentation involves manipulations of artificially induced conditions. Furthermore, the highly unnatural laboratory environment invariably stresses the animals, and stress affects the entire organism by altering pulse, blood pressure, hormone levels, immunological activities, and myriad other functions. . . .

Animal tests frequently mislead. Milrinone increased survival of rats with artificially induced heart failure, but humans taking this drug experienced a 30% increase in mortality. Fialuridine appeared safe in animal tests, but it caused liver failure in 7 of 15 humans taking the drug, five of whom died and two required liver transplantation. Animal studies failed to predict the dangerous heart valve abnormalities in humans induced by the diet drugs fenfluramine and dexfenfluramine.

Hormone replacement therapy increased women's risk of heart disease, breast cancer, and stroke, but experiments with mice, rabbits, pigs, and monkeys had predicted the opposite effect. The widely prescribed arthritis painkiller Vioxx, which was withdrawn from the global market in 2004 after causing an estimated 320,000 heart attacks, strokes, and causes of heart failure worldwide, 140,000 of them fatal, appeared safe and even beneficial to the heart in animal tests. David Graham, the Associate Director for Science and Medicine in the Office of Drug Safety at the FDA, described Vioxx as the "single greatest drug safety catastrophe in the history of this country or the history of the world." Animal tests also failed to predict the cases of partial or total blindness suffered by men taking the popular impotence drug Viagra. Despite mandatory, extensive animal testing, adverse drug reactions remain the fifth leading cause of mortality in the United States, accounting for more than 100,000 deaths per year. . . .

Scientists recognize that, even between humans, gender, ethnicity, age, and health can profoundly influence drug effects. Perhaps the most striking example of the specificity of drug effects comes from the demonstration that even human monozygotic twins display different drug responses, and that such responses become more disparate as the twins age. Obviously, extrapolating data between species is much more hazardous than within a species. Indeed, according to the FDA, a staggering 92% of all the drugs found safe and therapeutically effective in animal tests fail during human clinical trials due to their toxicity and/or inefficacy, and are therefore not approved. Furthermore, over half of the mere 8% which do gain FDA approval must be later withdrawn or relabeled due to severe, unexpected side effects.

The Value of Redirecting Research

The value of animal experimentation has been grossly exaggerated by those with a vested economic interest in its preservation. Because animal experimentation focuses on artificially created pathology, involves confounding variables, and is undermined by differences in human and nonhuman anatomy, physiology, and pathology, it is an inherently unsound method to investigate human disease processes. The billions of dollars invested annually in animal research would be put to much more efficient, effective, and humane use if redirected to clinical and epidemiological research and public health programs.

> "Animal experimentation has been the foundation for medical advances that have literally changed the world."

Drug Testing on Animals Is Beneficial

Jennifer A. Hurley

In the following viewpoint Jennifer Hurley asserts that animal experimentation is vital in fighting diseases such as AIDS. Jennifer Hurley writes and edits reference books for young adults.

As you read, consider the following questions:

1. How did animal research help create a polio vaccine?
2. How is animal experimentation better than in vitro research?
3. According to the author, why is animal testing vital to medical research?

When animal rights activists assert that animal experimentation does not save human lives, an obvious question comes to mind: Why would researchers choose to experiment on animals if it wasn't essential to medical progress? The answer is, of course, that they wouldn't. No scientist, researcher, or doctor enjoys experimenting on animals, especially if those experiments involve suffering. However, animal-based research is the only safe and effective way to develop the therapeutic drugs and medical procedures that save countless human lives. Would antivivisectionists really begrudge people their lives because a few animals had to die?

Eliminating the Plague of Polio

Animal experimentation has been the foundation for medical advances that have literally changed the world. Insulin for diabetes; organ, corneal, and bone marrow transplants; antibiotics for pneumonia; surgery for heart diseases; and the development of nonaddictive painkillers—all of these astounding medical breakthroughs were made possible through animal testing. Perhaps most significantly, the polio vaccine, given to every child in America, owes its existence to animal-based research. In the early 1950s, thousands of Americans, many of them children and young adults, were crippled or paralyzed by polio. Among the most hideous aspects of the disease was the iron lung, a huge steel breathing device that encased polio patients from the neck down. Some patients spent their entire lives inside an iron lung, with the ceiling as their only view of the world. Until the polio vaccine was introduced in 1961, parents were so afraid of their children catching the disease that "summer public beaches, playgrounds and movie theaters were places to be avoided." All of this ended when a vaccine for polio was developed through experimentation on monkeys. Albert Sabin, one of the researchers who developed the vaccine, claimed that "there could have been no oral polio vaccine without the use of innumerable animals, a very large number of animals." Today, animals are still needed to test the safety of each new batch of polio vaccine before it is given to children.

Animal Research and AIDS

Many researchers believe that animal-based research will eventually make acquired immunodeficiency syndrome (AIDS) as rare as polio is today. All of the treatments used to fight AIDS have been tested on animals. One experimental treatment involved the transplantation of baboon bone marrow cells into an AIDS patient. Once the transplant had been conducted, the baboon was killed painlessly with a lethal injection so that all of his tissues were available for future scientific study. Animal rights activists condemned the treatment, claiming it was wrong to kill the baboon. Would it have been right to let the AIDS patient die untreated? The sacrifice of any animal is unfortunate, but if that sacrifice saves human lives, it is completely justified. Not only do animal transplants have the potential to save AIDS patients, but they also have enormous possibilities for leukemia and lymphoma patients, who frequently go without transplants because of the lack of donors. Most importantly, almost all scientists believe that animal experiments are essential to finding an AIDS vaccine; in fact, one researcher asserts that excessively restrictive animal rights laws are the biggest obstacle to AIDS research. And, according to Joseph E. Murray, the 1990 Nobel Laureate in medicine, "Whenever a cure for AIDS is found, it will be through animal research."

No Alternative to Animals

Animal rights activists sometimes contend that, since almost all disease can be effectively prevented by a healthy lifestyle, medical research is unnecessary. It would certainly be nice if this were true. Unfortunately, prevention only plays a small part in combating disease because many illnesses are either due to genetic factors or their causes remain unknown. Disease prevention can never eliminate the need for medical research, and medical research will always need animals.

The study of human cell cultures, also referred to as in vitro research, has been touted as a viable alternative to animal experimentation; after all, say animal activists, what could be a better model for humans than actual human cells? How-

The U.S. Government's Opinion on Animal Testing

Animal testing by manufacturers seeking to market new products may be used to establish product safety. In some cases, after considering available alternatives, companies may determine that animal testing is necessary to assure the safety of a product or ingredient. FDA [Food and Drug Administration] supports and adheres to the provisions of applicable laws, regulations, and policies governing animal testing, including the Animal Welfare Act and the Public Health Service Policy of Humane Care and Use of Laboratory Animals. Moreover, in all cases where animal testing is used, FDA advocates that research and testing derive the maximum amount of useful scientific information from the minimum number of animals and employ the most humane methods available within the limits of scientific capability.

We also believe that prior to use of animals, consideration should be given to the use of scientifically valid alternative methods to whole-animal testing. In 1997, FDA joined with thirteen other Federal agencies in forming the Interagency Coordinating Committee on the Validation of Alternative Methods (ICCVAM). ICCVAM and its supporting center, the National Toxicology Program Interagency Center for the Evaluation of Alternative Toxicological Methods (NICEATM), coordinate the development, validation, acceptance, and harmonization of alternative toxicological test methods throughout the U.S. Federal Government. The ICCVAM/NICEATM mission statement indicates that these organizations "focus efforts on alternatives that may improve toxicity characterization, increase savings in time and cost, and even refine, reduce, or replace animal use."

Center for Food Safety and Applied Nutrition, "Animal Testing," April 5, 2006. www.cfsan.fda.gov.

ever, in vitro research has limitations. A cell culture cannot tell us the effects a drug will have on an entire human body, nor can it help doctors develop new surgical procedures. Computer-based approaches to medical research also have limitations. As David Hubel, the 1981 Nobel Prize winner in medicine states, "You can't train a heart surgeon on a computer, and to study a brain, you need a brain; a man-made machine is no substitute."

In the United States, we are so accustomed to the amenities of modern medicine that we take them for granted. All of our prescription drugs, medical procedures, cosmetics, and household products have undergone animal tests to assure their safety. Because of the medical progress made possible by animal research, we live in a world in which disease no longer threatens us at every moment, and most illnesses are completely curable. According to the American Association for Laboratory Animal Science, "There is not a person in the United States who has not somehow benefited from the results of research involving animals." Without the medical breakthroughs gained through animal experimentation, many of the animal rights activists who vehemently protest vivisection would not be around to voice their opinions. Perhaps there will be a day when medicine is so advanced that the use of animals will be superfluous; however, until every American is healthy, we cannot abandon the use of animals in research.

"It has been known among scientists and the pharmaceutical industry for decades that animal testing is scientifically unreliable."

Drug Testing on Animals Is Not Beneficial

Kathy Archibald

Kathy Archibald is the science director for Europeans for Medical Progress, a nonprofit organization that insists most animal experimentation is valueless and delays medical advances. In the following viewpoint, Archibald claims that drug testing on animals is done for legal reasons, not for scientific ones. That is, drug companies perform tests of new drugs on animals to convince the public that the drugs are safe and to protect themselves from legal liability if the drugs are later proven dangerous. Many licensed drugs do harm humans, Archibald notes, and such dangers are not always apparent in animal test subjects. Therefore, there is no scientific basis for continuing animal tests, Archibald maintains.

Kathy Archibald, "Animal Testing: Science or Fiction?" *Ecologist*, vol. 35, no. 4, May 2005, pp. 14–16. Copyright © 2005 MIT Press Journals. Reproduced by permission.

As you read, consider the following questions:

1. According to Archibald's article, what drug's release was referred to as the "single greatest drug-safety catastrophe in the history of the world" and why?
2. In the author's view, why are pharmaceutical companies "pragmatic" in selecting species to test drugs on?
3. What is "microdosing," as Archibald explains it, and how could it reduce animal testing?

M ost of us know that cancer, heart disease and stroke are the leading causes of death in the West. But many people would be surprised by the next biggest killer: side effects of prescription medicines. Adverse drug reactions kill more than 10,000 people a year in the UK (and more than 100,000 in the US), costing the NHS [National Health Service of England] alone £466m[illion] per year.

The pharmaceutical establishment constantly reassures us that all drugs are tested for safety and efficacy on animals before they can be administered to humans. When challenged about the ethics of vivisection, their defence typically goes like this: 'Which do you think is more important: your child's life or a rat's?' Given this choice most people would thankfully sacrifice the rat.

Animal Testing Fails

But what if you were told that the current animal testing procedures are seriously flawed? Consider the following evidence:

- Arthritis drug Vioxx, withdrawn from the global market in September 2004, appeared to be safe and even beneficial to the heart in animals, but caused as many as 140,000 heart attacks and strokes in the US alone. The associate safety director of the US Food and Drug Administration (FDA) described it as the 'single greatest drug-safety catastrophe in the history of the world'.

- Many studies published in the scientific literature comparing drug side effects in humans and animals have found animal tests to be less predictive than tossing a coin. One review of human-animal correlation in drugs that had been withdrawn because of adverse reactions found that animal tests predicted the human side effects only six out of 114 times.

- Hundreds of drugs to treat strokes (eg, Cerestat, Maxi-Post, Zendra, Lotrafiban, gavestinel, nimodipine, clomethiazole) have been found safe and effective in animal studies and then injured or killed patients in clinical trials.

- Hormone-replacement therapy (HRT), prescribed to many millions of women because it lowered monkeys' risk of heart disease and stroke, increases women's risks of these conditions significantly. The chairman of the German Commission on the Safety of Medicines described HRT as 'the new thalidomide'. In August 2003 *The Lancet* estimated that HRT had caused 20,000 cases of breast cancer over the past decade in Britain, in addition to many thousands of heart attacks and strokes.

- Dr. Richard Klausner, former director of the US National Cancer Institute (NCI), lamented: 'The history of cancer research has been a history of curing cancer in the mouse. We have cured mice of cancer for decades, and it simply didn't work in humans.' The NCI also believes we have lost cures for cancer because they were ineffective in mice.

- Cigarette smoke, asbestos, arsenic, benzene, alcohol and glass fibres are all safe to ingest, according to animal studies.

- Of 22 drugs shown to have been therapeutic in spinal cord injury in animals, not one is effective in humans.

- Of 20 compounds known not to cause cancer in humans, 19 do cause cancer in rodents.

- Dr. Albert Sabin, the inventor of the polio vaccine, swore under oath that the vaccine 'was long delayed by the erroneous conception of the nature of the human disease based on misleading experimental models of [it] in monkeys'.

- Penicillin, the world's first antibiotic, was delayed for more than l0 years by misleading results from experiments in rabbits, and would have been shelved forever had it been tested on guinea pigs, which it kills. [The discoverer of penicillin] Sir Alexander Fleming himself said: 'How fortunate we didn't have these animal tests in the 1940s, for penicillin would probably never have been granted a licence, and possibly the whole field of antibiotics might never have been realised.'

- Thalidomide, the infamous cause of birth defects in more than 10,000 children in the early 1960s, induces birth defects in very few species. Dr. James Schardein, the doyen of birth defect studies, says: 'In approximately 10 strains of rats, 15 strains of mice, 11 breeds of rabbits, two breeds of dogs, three strains of hamsters, eight species of primates, and in other such varied species as cats, armadillos, guinea pigs, swine and ferrets in which thalidomide has been tested, teratogenic effects [i.e., those that cause birth defects] have been induced only occasionally.' Ironically, if thalidomide, the drug whose side effects made animal testing obligatory, were assessed exclusively on its results in such tests it would still be passed today.

Even the *Handbook of Laboratory Animal Science* admits that 'uncritical reliance on the results of animal tests can be dangerously misleading and has cost the health and lives of tens of thousands of humans'.

Animal Tests Provide Liability Protection

Animal testing became legally enshrined in response to the thalidomide tragedy. The UK Medicines Act 1968 followed the US Kefauver-Harris Act, which was implemented in 1961 in the midst of the thalidomide furor to ensure that the FDA received proof of safety and efficacy for all new drugs. The intention was good but the reliance placed on animal tests to ensure safety was tragically ill-informed.

It has been known among scientists and the pharmaceutical industry for decades that animal testing is scientifically unreliable. As long ago as September 1962 *The Lancet* commented: 'We must face the fact that the most careful tests of a new drug's effects on animals may tell us little of its effect in humans.' In 1964 Dr. J. Gallagher, the medical director of Lederle Laboratories, admitted: 'Animal studies are done for legal reasons and not for scientific reasons.'

So, pharmaceutical companies conduct animal tests simply to satisfy government regulators. Crucially, animal data also provide liability protection when drugs kill or injure people. Industry can point to the rigorous animal tests they have performed and claim that they have done their best to ensure against tragedies occurring, thus minimising any damages awarded against them.

From the perspective of satisfying the regulators, pragmatic selection of species will demonstrate whatever is required of a drug, whether it is favourable safety or efficacy. And companies are not required to submit all their animal data, but only that from any two species (one rodent and one higher mammal). Dr. Irwin Bross, former director of the world's largest cancer research institute, the Sloan-Kettering, observed: 'Whenever government agencies or polluting corporations want to cover up an environmental hazard, they can always find an animal study to "prove" their claim. They can even do a new animal study which will come out the way they want by choosing the "right" animal model system.'

Killer Drugs

Many drugs that have been pronounced safe on the basis of animal tests have gone on to injure or kill people. For example:

- Vioxx, for arthritis, caused up to 60,000 deaths between its launch in 1999 and its withdrawal in 2004;

- Baycol (Lipobay), used to treat cholesterol, caused more than 10,000 cases of serious muscle-wasting or death between 1997 and its withdrawal in 2001;

- Rezulin (troglitazone), for diabetes, killed more than 400 people between 1997 and its withdrawal in 2000;

- Propulsid (cisapride), for heartburn, killed more than 300 adults and children before being withdrawn in 2000;

- Opren, for arthritis, caused 61 deaths and 3,500 serious injuries and was withdrawn in the 1980s;

- Eraldin, a heart treatment, killed 23 people and blinded many more, and was withdrawn in the 1970s. Its devastating side effects were not reproducible in any species except man;

- Isoprenaline, for asthma, killed 3,500 young people in Britain alone and was withdrawn in the 1960s. Intensive studies with rats, guinea pigs, dogs and monkeys, at huge dosages, failed to elicit similar results.

Kathy Archibald, "Animal Testing: Science or Fiction?"
Ecologist, vol. 35, no. 4, May 2005, pp. 14–16.

Avoiding More Extensive Clinical Trials

Placing massive emphasis on animal-safety data has also allowed pharmaceutical companies to avoid the expense of conducting clinical trials as extensively as they should. Since the

1950s doctors have been saying that clinical trials should involve more people, last for a longer period of time and use representatives of a broader swathe of society than the young, white males of standard practice. Women are generally not utilised in case they might be pregnant: the manufacturer would be held liable for any unanticipated birth defects. Very often trials do not even include representatives of the patient population the drug is designed to treat. This absurd situation clearly needs to be addressed.

There is no getting away from the fact that people have to be the ultimate guinea pigs for testing new treatments. Clearly, the health and safety of research volunteers and patients should be paramount and the best safeguards should be in place to protect them.

Alternatives Are Available

New drugs go through three basic testing phases: in vitro (test-tube) and in silico (computer) modelling; animal testing; and, finally, human trials.

Before a drug is tested in humans, there should be persuasive evidence that it is safe and effective. No method, neither animal, human nor test-tube, can predict the reactions of every patient with 100 per cent accuracy. Reactions differ between sexes, ages, ethnic groups, even between family members. We are all different, but not as different from each other as we are from animals, with which the differences are so great that they render extrapolation hazardous. Non-animal methods are not completely fail-safe, but do offer more security.

There are excellent in silico and in vitro testing methods available today. Many companies specialise in virtual screening or drugs for potential toxic effects. A wide range of predictive software is available, including complete clinical trial simulations. Other companies focus on safety and efficacy assessments in human tissues. A 10-year international study proved that human cell culture tests are more accurate and yield more useful information about toxic mechanisms than traditional animal tests.

In place of animal-based pre-clinical studies, subsequent clinical trial patients and volunteers would be better protected by the adoption of preliminary microdosing studies (or 'phase 0' clinical trials). Microdose studies involve the administration of ultra-small (and safe) doses of the test drug to volunteers monitored by scanners. Human microdosing, based on the concept that the best model for man is man, helps in selecting the best drug candidates before advancing into full development, thereby reducing the chances of failure in later, more risky and more expensive phases.

During clinical trials, relevant pharmacological measurements should be made, which would give early warning of potential problems. It is true that some rare side effects will only be detected when drugs are prescribed to large numbers of people. This is why post-marketing drug surveillance is so important and should be strengthened, in order to pick up these effects as quickly as possible. Reports of adverse reactions to drugs are currently soaring in the US, where a record 422,500 adverse events were reported to the FDA in 2004. The FDA cautions that the actual number is likely to be between 10 and 100 times greater because of under-reporting.

"*[A microchip] system could not only replace conventional cell cultures but also reduce a reliance on animal experiments.*"

Microchip Technologies Could Make Drug Testing on Animals Unnecessary

David H. Freedman

In the following viewpoint David H. Freedman, a freelance journalist, states that a technological breakthrough could make animal drug testing unnecessary. As Freedman writes, scientists are merging human tissue cultures with microchips to create minute replicas of human internal systems. These miniature systems are better able to predict the effects of untried drugs on human physiology than charting the reactions of animals to such drugs. Researchers are hopeful, Freedman reports, that the new microchip testing methods will thus reduce the need for extensive, wasteful, and often inconclusive animal testing.

As you read, consider the following questions:

1. According to Freedman, why are drug companies eager to obtain the new "animal on a chip" testing devices?

David H. Freedman, "The Silicon Guinea Pig," *Technology Review*, vol. 107, June 2004, pp. 62–69. © 2004 by the Association of Alumni and Alumnae of MIT. Reproduced by permission.

2. As the author reports, why are traditional cell-culture tests not always accurate?

3. Using the naphthalene example, explain how Michael Shuler's chip model detected toxicity problems that traditional cell cultures could not.

Michael Shuler's chip could pass for any small silicon slab pried out of a computer or cell phone. Which makes it seem all the more out of place on a bench top in the Cornell University researcher's lab, surrounded by petri dishes, beakers, and other bio-clutter and mounted in a plastic tray like a dissected mouse. The chip appears to be on some sort of life support, with pinkish fluid pumping into it through tubes. Shuler methodically points out the components of the chip with a pencil: here's the liver, the lungs are over here, this is fat. He then injects an experimental drug into the imitation blood coursing through these "organs" and "tissues"—actually tiny mazes of twisting pipes and chambers lined with living cells. The compound will react with other chemicals, accumulate in some of the organs, and pass quickly through others. After several hours, Shuler and his team will be closer to answering a key question: is the compound, when given to an actual human, likely to do more harm than good?

This so-called animal on a chip was designed to help overcome an enormous obstacle to discovering new drugs: there is currently no quick, reliable way to predict if an experimental compound will have toxic side effects—if it will make people sick instead of making them well. Testing in animals is the best drug-makers can do, but it is slow, expensive, often inaccurate, and objectionable to many. To minimize the number of animal tests, drug companies routinely screen drug candidates using cell cultures—essentially clumps of living human or animal cells growing in petri dishes or test tubes. The approach is relatively cheap and easy, but it gives only a hazy prediction of what will happen to a compound on the circuitous trip through the tissues and organs of an animal.

Eagerly Anticipated Technology

Shuler is among a handful of researchers who are developing more sophisticated cell cultures that simulate the body's complex organs and tissues. MIT [Massachusetts Institute of Technology] tissue engineer Linda Griffith, for one, has built a chip that mimics some of the functions of a liver, while Shuichi Takayama, a biomedical engineer at the University of Michigan, has built one that imitates the behavior of the vasculatory system. But while such efforts have produced convincing analogues of parts of human or animal bodies, Shuler has gone a step further. Working with colleague Greg Baxter, who launched Beverly Hills, CA-based Hurel to commercialize the technology, Shuler has combined replicas of multiple animal organs on a single chip, creating a rough stand-in for an entire mammal. Other versions of Shuler's chips attempt to go even further, using human cells to more faithfully reproduce the effects of a compound in the body.

Drug companies are interested, and no wonder: they routinely make thousands, even tens of thousands, of compounds in hopes of finding one that is effective against a particular target. Chips such as Shuler and Baxter's could mean a cheap, fast, and accurate way to weed out compounds that would eventually prove toxic, saving companies years and millions of dollars on the development of worthless drugs. According to a recent study by Tufts University's Center for the Study of Drug Development, for each drug that reaches market, the drug industry spends an average of $467 million on human testing—the vast majority of the money going to drugs that fail, either because they aren't effective or because they prove toxic. If more failures could be identified before animal testing even began, companies could focus more of their time and money on the winners. "Everyone in the industry hopes to have surrogates for animals and humans when it comes to testing compounds" says Jack Reynolds, head of safety sciences for Pfizer, the world's largest pharmaceutical firm. "This is the sort of technology we'd want in our toolbox." . . .

Replicating Human Systems

When a person takes a drug, its active ingredient goes on a wild ride to get to the target cells: it might be absorbed by the gut, broken down by enzymes in the liver, hoarded for weeks by fat cells, screened out by a brain membrane, and whirled through the whole ordeal over and over again by the blood. When that happens, an otherwise harmless compound can accumulate in a particular organ until it reaches toxic levels. Or it can be transformed into a different compound altogether, which itself is toxic. Pfizer's Reynolds estimates that, of drug candidates that end up proving unsafe, approximately 40 percent acquire their toxicity after being converted to other compounds in the body.

One reason that conventional cell-culture tests often mislead researchers is that they don't present the complex brew of enzymes and other chemicals that a drug can encounter and react with in the various tissues of the body. And simple cell cultures don't reveal how much of a drug actually gets to different types of cells, in what form, and for how long. Indeed, nearly half of the drugs that seem safe in cell-culture testing prove toxic in animal tests; and even more fail when they encounter the complex tissues and organs of humans. Researchers hope, however, that cell cultures that better simulate the conditions in the body will do a far better job at spotting toxic drugs, reducing the reliance on animal and human testing. . . .

Testing in Miniature

Michael Shuler is a 57-year-old, lanky chemical engineering professor who has nurtured a side interest in biological pro-

Singer. © 2005 Andrew B. Singer, www.andysinger.com. Reproduced by permission.

cesses since junior high school. By 1989 he had become interested in toxicity testing, and he had been pondering the unreliability of conventional cell cultures when an idea occurred to him: could you make a cell culture that replicates the journey through the various organs? He recognized it as a chemical engineering problem: glass chambers lined with different types of cells and hooked up via tubes to each other and to a pump that sent fluid through them would far more realistically simulate a body, and tests employing them might predict what happens in living animals much more accurately.

After several months, Shuler and students had constructed a bench-top conglomeration of cells and plumbing providing a crude working model of a set of mammalian organs. It sort of functioned, but Shuler knew there was a big problem with its fidelity: almost all of the chemistry in the body takes place in tissues packed with minute canals and chambers, where critical reactions hinge on the ability of various chemicals to concentrate in some places and diffuse in others, depending in part on the microscopic geography. Mixing everything up in big beakers would distort that delicate balance. Plus, at this size the system wouldn't be practical or cheap enough for large-scale testing.

Meanwhile, molecular biologist Greg Baxter had just joined Cornell's Nanobiotechnology Center as a research scientist. His specialty was microfluidics—essentially, microscopic plumbing on a chip. On his second day he buttonholed Shuler at his lab, wondering if he had any projects that could benefit from ultraminiaturization. Funny you should ask, said Shuler.

It took just two meetings to hammer out the basic chip design and a year to produce the first prototype. To build one of the devices, the researchers carve minute trenches that look like faint scratches into a thumbnail-sized silicon chip; these trenches serve as fluid-carrying pipes. Producing microfluidic features on chips for testing chemical reactions and imitating biological processes is not new. But by combining their skills in chemical engineering and microfabrication, Shuler and Baxter add a significant twist: they've engineered the sizes, lengths, and layout of all the trenches in an attempt to closely duplicate the fluid flows and chemical exposures that cells experience in real organs. . . .

After a test compound has circulated through the chip for several hours, the cells in the chip are monitored, either with a microscope or via embedded sensors that can test for oxygen and other indicators. Do the cells absorb the compound? Does it sicken or kill them? As in an actual animal, each organ or tissue plays a specific role in the chip. The liver and gut break some compounds down into smaller molecules, for example, while the fat—jammed not only with cells, but also with a spongelike gel—often retains compounds, allowing them to leak out later. A "target" organ or tissue is usually included to demonstrate the ultimate effects of the compound; this might be a cancer tumor, or an especially vulnerable tissue, such as the lung's, or bone marrow.

Early Signs Are Encouraging

The chips, of course, will have to be extensively tested before drug firms will use them widely. Still, early signs are encouraging. Shuler ran one experiment with naphthalene, a compound used in mothballs and pesticides. Excessive exposure causes lung damage, but you wouldn't know it from standard cell-culture tests. That's because the culprit isn't naphthalene itself but rather two chemicals produced by the liver when it breaks naphthalene down. If you knew that and splashed those by-products directly on lung cells in culture, you'd observe such a severe response that you'd conclude even slight exposure to naphthalene is extremely dangerous. But that's wrong, too; as it turns out, fat cells yank much of the toxic compounds out of the system. Shuler's chip convincingly mimics this chain of events, yielding a realistic measure of the damage.

Such precise simulation promises to help drug companies improve their screening of drug candidates—and waste less time and money on those that will ultimately rail animal tests. According to Baxter, the chips are ready for such an application right now, and six large companies are currently talking to Hurel about adopting the technology [Johnson & Johnson has since entered into collaboration with Hurel]. Shuler aided by a team of students and collaborators at Cornell and elsewhere, is working on further shrinking and automating the technology. The goal: a sheet-of-paper-sized bank of 96 chips that plugs into a robotic lab setup that very rapidly adds test drugs and monitors the results. The system could not only replace conventional cell cultures but also reduce a reliance on animal experiments, in which researchers must use a great number of animals to test different doses of a drug, and must monitor those animals over time to pick up subtle side effects. "We're talking about running a test in one or two days that would take months with animals," says Shuler. Shuler projects a per-chip production price of about $50 complete with cells, compared to the hundreds or even thousands of dollars it takes to acquire and maintain a single lab animal.

Replacing Animals

Chips that replicate the functioning of animals will likely be the first versions of the technology to make a commercial impact. But the hope is that once those prove to accurately predict the results of animal tests, human-on-a-chip versions will provide a good indication of how toxic a drug is likely to prove in human trials.

Animal testing plays that role now, but not very well. Four out of five drugs that make it through animal testing end up failing in human clinical trials, usually because of safety concerns. Part of the problem is that mice can't tell you they have headaches, blurred vision, or stomach cramps. But the larger issue is simply that animals' organs, and the processes that take place in them, are not identical to those of humans. No one knows how many drugs that would have been safe in humans were shelved because they sickened some animals. (Penicillin, for instance, is toxic to guinea pigs but fortunately was also tested on mice.) . . .

Neither Baxter nor Shuler claims that the animal on a chip is any sort of panacea for the complex and deeply challenging drug-development process. For one thing, the chips still have to prove in large-scale tests that they really do a better job than conventional cell cultures of predicting toxicity. But if they measure up, then the pills you take ten years from now may very well arrive thanks to the sacrifices of a silicon lab rat.

Periodical Bibliography

The following articles have been selected to supplement the diverse views presented in this chapter.

Celeste Biever	"Can Computer Models Replace Animal Testing?" *New Scientist*, May 13, 2006.
Bernadine Healy	"The Tribulation of Trials," *U.S. News & World Report*, April 3, 2006.
Lancet	"Animal Research Is a Source of Human Compassion, Not Shame," September 4, 2004.
Graham Lappin	"Animal Experimentation, the Worst Form of Science?" *Biologist*, April 2004.
New York Times	"Why Test Animals to Cure Human Depression?" March 28, 2004.
Ellen Frankel Paul	"Why Animal Experimentation Matters," *Society*, September–October 2002.
Katherine Perlo	"'Would You Let Your Child Die Rather than Experiment on Nonhuman Animals?' A Comparative Questions Approach," *Society & Animals*, March 2003.
Amanda Schupak	"The Bunny Chip," *Forbes*, August 15, 2005.
Science News	"Frankenstein's Chips," *Science News*, January 8, 2005.
Richard Smith	"Animal Research: The Need for a Middle Ground," *British Medical Journal*, February 3, 2001.
Barry Yeoman	"Can We Trust Research Done with Lab Mice?" *Discover*, July 2003.

OPPOSING
VIEWPOINTS®
SERIES

CHAPTER 4

Are New Forms of Animal Experimentation Worth Pursuing?

Chapter Preface

In December 2004, Genetic Savings and Clone, a San Francisco cloning and technology firm, made the first sale of a cloned house cat to a buyer in Texas. Since then, other biotechnology operations have been banking animal DNA with the prospect of following Genetic Savings and Clone's lead. The service typically costs between $300 and $1000 for the initial cryogenic freezing of animal cells, and around $100 per year for maintenance. To have a clone made, the price jumps to $50,000, so many clients are banking their beloved pets' cells until the price for the cloning procedure drops as the technology improves.

Some animal rights activists are disheartened by this aspect of the new cloning industry because they believe it is driven by human vanity and not a love for pets. After all, clones are only physical duplicates of the original animals; they do not have the same personality or habits of their progenitors. Animal activists suggest that copying pets is unnecessary given the fact that animal shelters destroy millions of animals each year because not enough people can be found to adopt them. Other critics simply find the notion of cloning so off-putting that they condemn the science as monstrous.

Cloning has met less resistance in the agricultural market. Cattle breeders, for example, have already introduced cloned cows into their herds. The cost is far less expensive than cat cloning (because cow eggs are easier to obtain in large numbers from slaughterhouses), so the economics of cloning cattle makes sense. The U.S. Food and Drug Administration has yet to allow markets to carry beef from cloned cattle; copied cows are therefore mainly used for breeding. Bio, a Web site organization that champions the biotechnology industry, explains that "the breeding technique allows a greater number of farmers the ability to preserve and extend proven, superior genetics. Ranchers would also be able to select and propagate the best animals—beef cattle that are fast-growing, have lean but tender meat, and are disease-resistant." Other livestock—such as goats and sheep—can and have also been cloned, but the economic constraints and the lack of demand for duplicating these animals has not made cloning them attractive.

Cloned cattle and other livestock can also contribute to the field of biomedicine. Genetically modified cows, for example, have been engineered to produce human antibodies that can then be administered to people in the form of vaccines. The modified cows could then be duplicated to yield more and more of these antibody factories. In a 2005 article in the *Scientist*, Jim Robl, the president of the Connecticut-based cloning firm Hematech, maintained, "Once you've got the production system in place, you can use the same system to immunize with any number of different antigens."

Cloning is one of the scientific breakthroughs debated in the following chapter. Other forms of genetically manipulating animals are also discussed. Such cutting-edge technologies have greatly expanded the arguments for and against animal experimentation and will likely continue to shape the debate as advances are made in the near future.

| "Patients with a pig organ may be in-
herently vulnerable to infections transmitted from the pig organ itself."

The Risks of Animal-to-Human Transplants Outweigh the Benefits

Joyce D'Silva

*Joyce D'Silva is an ambassador for Compassion in World Farm-
ing, an anti–animal cruelty organization that opposes factory
farming. In the following viewpoint she claims that people are
too eager to extend their lives. The newest medical promise, she
asserts, is to replace failing human organs with healthy pig organs. Such a fix does not come without risks, however. According
to D'Silva, the pig organs may carry dangerous viruses. Furthermore, in experiments using primate recipients, the pig transplant
organs have been rejected by the hosts' immune systems. To continue these experiments in hopes of prolonging life, D'Silva argues, is not worth the risks nor the suffering it brings to the animals involved.*

As you read, consider the following questions:

1. What is xenozoonosis, as D'Silva defines it?

Joyce D'Silva, "Dying to Live," *Chemistry and Industry*, December 4, 2000, p. 767.
Copyright © 2000 Society of Chemical Industry. Reproduced by permission.

2. According to D'Silva, what kind of genetic modifications will likely be performed on donor pigs?

3. In what way does D'Silva have a personal connection to the issue of longevity?

You would think we could live forever, one day. All our expectations of medical research, all our obsessions with health and diet, even the potential of cryopreserved corpses could lead us to believe our finite, physical bodies are capable of infinite life, one day.

Hit the right spot on my genome, tweak a bit here, eliminate there and, who knows, one day?

Media headlines fuel our hopes with promises of cures for the whole range of diseases to which we may succumb, one day.

We may dream of larger houses, cottages in the country, Caribbean holidays or faster, larger cars, but, most of all, we desire our own longevity. It's as if length of chronological time is somehow a bonus in itself, quantity being the criterion for the good life, not quality.

How attached to life we are. How bound up with our careers, our homes, our hobbies and, of course, our loved ones and ourselves.

We would risk much to preserve our own personal status quo—and that includes our own physical ability to breathe and think and function. We will risk dangerous operations, because there's a chance of success. We'll willingly try new treatments, because they may work. We'll try out alternative therapies, because they may hold some ancient secret of life (and they will, usually, at least make us feel better).

And soon, there'll be a new quick-fix coming to a hospital near you: the promise of an animal heart for your failing one, a pig kidney, a pair of lungs, a liver and who knows what other organs from an animal, one day.

The Danger of Viral Disease

Patients with a pig organ may be inherently vulnerable to infections transmitted from the pig organ itself. Research has shown human cells can be infected by porcine endogenous retroviruses. What has been found in the laboratory may be even more easily replicated in the intimacy of the body.

But viruses are masters of mobility and, in a new host, they can be devastating, viz. AIDS. One person, the xenotransplant patient, is unlikely to be the end-point of their activity; they'll be spreading to family, friends and the rest of us. This is not hype. American researchers have already coined a new term for an animal disease transmitted to a xenotransplant recipient (and beyond?)—'xenozoonosis'.

These pigs will be no ordinary pigs, although almost certainly they will share the ability to enjoy life or to suffer along with all other pigs. But these are humano-pigs, genetically engineered to reduce the likelihood of their organs being rejected. Genetic engineering is still such a hit-and-miss procedure with a minute 'success' rate, that the pigs will likely be cloned too.

A huge number of female pigs will be operated on to remove egg cells for genetic modification and cloning work. Others will be operated on for implantation of the genetically modified (GM) or cloned embryos.

We know genetic engineering has produced gross malformations in many pigs, and we know cloned farm animals are frequently abnormal and die within days or are aborted before birth. We know strict hygiene requirements mean the GM piglets will be born by specific pathogen-free methods, that is hysterectomy and fatal injection for mother and sterile rearing conditions for her orphans. During their lives, repeated blood and tissue tests may be followed up by the removal of organs in sequence, while keeping the animal alive in 'hospital' conditions.

Viral Dangers of Pig Organs

Current xenotransplantation hopes are focused on pigs. Pigs, like other animals, carry bacteria and "exogenous" viruses (viruses that happen to infect particular animals). It would be premature to presume that we already know everything about pig viruses; for instance, a new virus related to human hepatitis E was reported in pigs in 1998. Many bacteria infect both pigs and humans, and human recipients of pig heart valves have been infected by *Myocardium fortuitum* complex. Pigs also harbor many viruses that could be transmitted to humans, some of which might be far more damaging to us than to their usual hosts.

Pigs also carry endogenous retroviruses (PERV), retroviruses whose DNA has become part of the pig genome. These are worrisome because retroviruses have exceptionally high mutation rates; they would also be difficult or impossible to eradicate. Pigs are also infected by many parasites. . . .

In short, several factors . . . render calculations of risk even less reliable than usual. These factors together could generate a catastrophic scenario in which a pig microorganism mutated into an easily transmissible, lethal, human disease. Such a microorganism might turn out to be unstoppable by any known treatment, and could, conceivably, threaten human existence altogether.

Laura Purdy, "Should We Add 'Xeno' to 'Transplantation'?"
Politics and Life Science, *vol. 19, no. 2, September 2000.*

As the [British] government's own expert committee [Advisory Group on the Ethics of Xenotransplantation] succinctly put it: 'We regret that animal suffering is caused but we conclude that these are inevitable compromises if xenotransplantation is to take place'. This committee made such a strong acknowledgement of the inevitability of the suffering of these source animals that they said it would be 'ethically unacceptable to use primates as source animals for xenotransplantation, not least because they would be exposed to too much suffering.

Failed Experiments

As for those primates, hundreds are already being used as recipients of GM pig organs. Experiment after experiment tells us how they suffer as their bodies reject the transplant, their immune systems are rendered useless and they succumb, if not to rejection, then to infection or poisoning.

Can these 'means' justify a possible 'end' for our own species, the tempting fantasy of a year or two more of life, of togetherness?

Seen in the round, it surely cries out: 'Unfair!', 'Too risky!' and 'Not worth it!'

And yet we ache for longevity. I know. I've seen my own husband struggle to live post stroke for three years until his death. We'd have tried anything to make his stumbling fingers virtuoso-like again on the guitar and to make his shaky legs strong so we could climb those hills again.

Animal organs or tissues weren't on offer. But if they had been, would we have opted for them? Maybe. But would we have been right? I think not.

I "If we never took risks with the unknown we would make little progress
in medicine."

The Benefits of
Animal-to-Human Transplants
Outweigh the Risks

A physician, interviewed by Gale Scott

The following viewpoint is a New York Times *interview with a
physician concerning the potential value of animal-to-human
organ transplants. The physician claims that xenotransplants
will soon ease the need for human organs, which are often from
older or less than ideal donors. The doctor acknowledges that science must first overcome the risks of viral infection and the high
cost of using animal organs. The speaker argues, however, that
the benefits of providing human patients with healthy animal
organs outweigh these risks. The interview was conducted by
health reporter Gale Scott.*

As you read, consider the following questions:

1. In the author's view, how do brain death and brain injury make human organs less ideal to donate?

2. What viruses does the doctor note are sometimes transferred during human-to-human transplants?

3. According to the doctor, why would patient tolerance to animal transplant organs lower the cost of such transplants?

The potential benefits of xenotransplantation, most likely using pig organs and tissues, are immense. Because of a shortage of donor organs, 50,000 of the 70,000 people in the United States who are awaiting transplants will not get them this year.

Those who need kidneys may remain on dialysis, but those needing a heart or liver stand a good chance of dying. If we had an unlimited supply of animal organs, patients could receive transplants while still in reasonable health.

We frequently have to wait until the heart and liver patients have deteriorated to the extent that they need to be in an intensive care unit.

If the transplant could be performed when first needed, patients would recover more rapidly and the associated costs would decrease.

A Better Kind of Organ

The quality of donor pig organs will certainly be better than those from human cadavers. Brain injury and brain death can stress organs, particularly the heart.

Some transplanted hearts fail to support the circulation adequately even though they looked good in the donor.

Also, the pressure on surgeons to save lives is such that they are increasingly being forced to use organs from elderly or less than ideal donors, where the organ may not be perfect.

Using specially bred and housed donor pigs gives us the potential to reduce many infections. Virtually every time we transplant a human organ, we knowingly transfer an infec-

Why Xenotransplantation Should Move Ahead

Both in the UK and USA, oversight agencies are . . . increasingly eager to continue with research concerning xenotransplantation. It is indeed conceivable that we are overestimating the magnitude of the problem. As we cannot currently predict the consequences of transplantation of a transgenic porcine organ into a human, we must also bear in mind the possibility that no transmission of dangerous, uncontrollable viruses will occur. In this case, many would find it immoral to deny such a life saving intervention if it is one day thought feasible. It would be questionable to still allow transplant teams to increasingly rely on problematic strategies to widen the donor pool, such as the use of organs from so called marginal donors. The use of organs from elderly donors and donors with a health condition is not an attractive alternative to the prospect of transplanting compatible, healthy porcine organs. Safe and effective xenotransplantation would not only resolve the current allograft shortage, it would also annul the high financial and emotional burdens associated with long waiting times for an available donor organ and allow for a precisely scheduled transplant, thereby overcoming many practical problems for the transplant team. Also, specially engineered pigs may one day provide suitable organs for infants, for whom the organ shortage is the most devastating.

A. Ravelingien et al., "Proceeding with Clinical Trials of Animal to Human Organ Transplantation: A Way Out of the Dilemma," Journal of Medical Ethics, *vol. 30, 2004.*

tious agent. That includes cytomegalovirus, Epstein-Barr virus and even the hepatitis viruses.

There will always be the risk of transferring a hitherto unknown infectious agent, although many of the measures we shall take to exclude known viruses are likely also to exclude unknown viruses, if present.

If we have excluded all known infectious agents we would be justified in proceeding with trials in patients.

Many groups are investigating whether there is a potential risk in transferring porcine endogenous viruses to humans. These viruses are present in every pig cell, yet there is no evidence that they are harmful to pigs or would be harmful to humans. But we need assurances.

We have a strain of pig in Boston that appears unable to transmit their viruses to human cells.

If this finding holds up, concerns about infecting the transplant recipient or the public may be diminished.

Reducing Costs

As for cost, organs from genetically engineered pigs may well cost several thousand dollars. But expenses now associated with procuring organs from human donors can range from $7,500 to $25,000. Successful transplants will mean savings on dialysis and other forms of treatment of patients with end-stage organ failure.

One further development may reduce costs.

My colleagues can now induce what is known as a state of tolerance in some patients receiving a human organ transplant, which means that they require no immunosuppressive drugs after the first few weeks. We are trying to induce tolerance to a transplanted pig organ.

If this could be achieved, it would not only be greatly beneficial for the patients, as they would avoid the side effects of drug therapy, but the long-term costs would be significantly reduced.

If we never took risks with the unknown we would make little progress in medicine.

| "More than 100 foreign proteins have been produced experimentally from different organs in several animal species."

Genetically Modified Animals Are Beneficial to Medicine

Part I: Alexandre Fouassier; Part II: Manufacturing Chemist

The following two viewpoints were taken from Manufacturing Chemist, *an international trade journal. In the first viewpoint Alexandre Fouassier, a development manager at BioProtein Technologies in Paris explains how insertion of human genetic material into rabbits can force the animals to express a desired protein. The protein is then harvested from the rabbits' milk. In the second viewpoint the staff of* Manufacturing Chemist *reports that the genetic modification of cows allows for the production of human antibodies within these animals. These two viewpoints argue that the creation of "transgenic" animals such as modified rabbits and cows will be useful in quickly producing human proteins and antibodies that can be used to fight disease.*

As you read, consider the following questions:

1. According to Fouassier, what diseases has the cloned erythroprotein been used to combat?

2. As Fouassier states, what advantages do transgenic animals offer pharmaceutical companies in the production of complex proteins?

3. According to *Manufacturing Chemist*, what two factors limit the supply of immunoglobulin, an antibody used in the treatment of many immune system disorders?

Part I

Over the past few years, biotechnology has generated new opportunities for the development of human pharmaceuticals. One particular success story is the use of recombinant technologies to produce therapeutically useful proteins, such as hormones, antibodies, growth factors and antigens for vaccines. Producing these proteins in the quantities required to meet clinical needs presents a challenge, however, and manufacturers are constantly looking for new solutions. Transgenic animals provide one answer, and can offer benefits compared with traditional methods of recombinant protein manufacture. The transgenic rabbit, in particular, gives a fast, cost-effective and efficient means of producing therapeutic protein in milk.

Through advances in biotechnological techniques, scientists are able to isolate sequences of bases coding for specific proteins (genes), and insert them into the DNA of other living cells. These 'hosts' are usually rapidly reproducing cells such as bacteria, yeast or cultured cell lines, which can be grown in large volumes to express the protein of interest on an industrial scale for use in therapeutics. Naturally occurring erythropoietin, for example, is a very rare glycoprotein hormone responsible for the regulation of red blood cell production. The erythropoietin gene was cloned in 1985 and today it is routinely expressed [i.e., developed] in cultured cells. The recombinant erythropoietin harvested from these cells is used to increase the production of red blood cells in patients with anaemia caused by a variety of conditions, such as cancer chemotherapy or in association with HIV. . . .

The use of transgenic animals and plants for the production of human therapeutic proteins is a relatively new manufacturing development. Ever since the birth of 'Tracey', in 1991, the first transgenic sheep expressing the human blood clotting factor, human a-1-antitypsin, the idea of transgenic animals as protein fermentors has taken off.

Since then, more than 100 foreign proteins have been produced experimentally from different organs in several animal species. Transgenic animals have the potential to make a significant contribution to the production of biopharmaceuticals because they can produce complex proteins at high volume and with low cost.

Methods of Transferring Genetic Material

Transgenic animals can be created through two principal methods—microinjection and nuclear transfer.

In the microinjection method, freshly fertilised oocytes [eggs] are harvested and DNA constructs [foreign genetic coding] are injected into the male pronucleus (a vacuole that contains the male DNA and has entered the female egg but has yet to fuse with the egg pronucleus) using a thin glass needle. The male and female pronuclei fuse to form the nucleus, which now contains foreign DNA. The cell then divides to form a two-cell embryo and is transferred into a recipient female.

The main disadvantage of this technique is that transgene integration within the male pronucleus genome is random. The expression of the transgene can, therefore, be affected by its position in the genome, meaning that the subsequent selection of efficient protein-producing animals is required.

Nuclear transfer involves transferring the nucleus from a somatic [nonreproductive] cell into an enucleated oocyte [one that has had its nucleus removed]. . . .

Choosing the Desired Protein and Its Source

The choice of animal for commercial protein production depends on a variety of factors, including generation time, number of offspring, potential yield and susceptibility to disease. A variety of animals have been used successfully, including mice, rabbits, goats, sheep and cows.

The source of the protein is also an important consideration. Milk, blood, urine and seminal plasma can be used, as well as the egg white from birds' eggs and the cocoons of some insects.

The most convenient source is milk, however. The secretory properties of the mammary gland make it the ideal protein producer, and the milk is easy to collect. . . .

In general, the larger the animal, the greater the milk yield, but this must be balanced against longer gestation periods and the time it takes to produce a functional transgenic herd. A key factor in the use of transgenic species is the efficiency of expression of the desired protein. . . . The rabbit has emerged as a key model for protein production based on: the speed at which transgenic animal colonies can be established; good milk yields; high protein content; an ability to produce complex functional proteins; and ease of handling.

Transgenic rabbits are generally produced using the microinjection method. A female rabbit is implanted with 20 viable embryos containing DNA constructs. The founder generation are born after one month. . . .

A Cost-Effective Option

The benefits of the rabbit are particularly important in light of today's uncertain manufacturing environments. Biotechnology-derived products represent about 25% of all new medicines and it is predicted that this will increase to about 50% within 10 years.

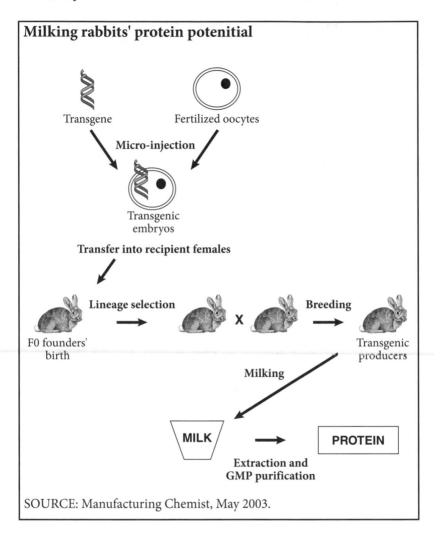

Milking rabbits' protein potenitial

Transgene   Fertilized oocytes

Micro-injection

Transgenic embryos

Transfer into recipient females

Lineage selection   X   **Breeding**

F0 founders' birth   Transgenic producers

Milking

MILK   PROTEIN

Extraction and GMP purification

SOURCE: Manufacturing Chemist, May 2003.

Current trends indicate that there is going to be a shortfall in manufacturing capacity for biopharmaceuticals. While many companies are investing in increasing their manufacturing capacity, it can take four to five years to build a manufacturing plant at a cost of US$100–500m[illion] ([euro]94.5-473m). The use of transgenics offers pharmaceutical and biotechnology companies an attractive option as a highly flexible, scaleable source of protein with a fast time to full production.

Part II

Cows Offer Potential New Source of Human Antibodies

Scientists have reported the successful application of proprietary cloning techniques to produce four calves that express a human chromosome fragment coding for the broad range of human antibodies. The research was the result of an ongoing joint effort between US company Hematech and Kirin Brewery to develop a system for the production of human polyclonal antibody-based therapeutics. This marks the first step in the development of a large-scale system for producing human polyclonal antibodies [antibodies derived from different cell lines] that could be used to prevent and/or treat a wide variety of diseases, including antibiotic resistant infections, autoimmune diseases, cancer and diseases resulting from bioterrorism.

Currently there is a substantial need for immunoglobulin [proteins secreted by plasma in the immune system], or broad-spectrum human polyclonal antibodies, for the treatment of many immune system disorders. However, the supply is limited to that which can be obtained from human donors and the application is limited because human donors cannot be optimally immunised.

'A bovine system for the production of human polyclonal antibodies would be fast and easily scalable to tons of product,' said Dr. James Robl, president and chief scientific officer of Hematech. 'A cow carrying complete human antibody genes could simply be immunised against the target disease agent and human antibodies could be collected in a couple of months.'

Meanwhile, the company has been awarded US$3.3m[illion] ([euro]3.1m) in government funding to develop a bovine system for producing human polyclonal antibodies against botulinum neurotoxins, which pose a major bioweapons threat. . . .

> *"Many if not most human proteins will not be 'as they should' structurally, functionally and biochemically unless they are produced in a human milieu."*

Genetically Modified Animals Are Not Beneficial to Medicine

Animal Aid

Animal Aid is a British organization that campaigns against cruelty to animals. In the following viewpoint Animal Aid asserts that genetically modified (GM) animals have not benefited medical progress. According to the organization, using GM animals as disease models has failed to yield results that can be applied to humans. In addition, the use of GM animals to produce beneficial human proteins has the potential of transmitting animal diseases to human recipients. In both cases, the suffering and harm to the animals involved also calls into question the necessity of such experiments.

Animal Aid, "Man or Mouse: Uses of, and Problems with, Genetically Modified Animals," Kent, United Kingdom: Animal Aid, 2005. www.animalaid.org.uk/viv/manmouse3.htmwww.animalaid.org.uk. Reproduced by permission.

As you read, consider the following questions:

1. According to Animal Aid, what percent of toxicity testing results done on one group of animals can be correlated by tests on other groups?

2. In Animal Aid's view, why are pharmaceutical companies investigating the use of GM animals to make human proteins when other production methods are available?

3. What is "leaky" gene expression and why does Animal Aid say it is problematic for GM animals?

If promises from those involved in their creation are to be believed, the contribution of GM animals to human life will rival that of the wheel. Manipulating the genomes of 'imperfect' animals will lead to a complete understanding of genetics and cell biology; drugs to cure all diseases; simple and reliable test protocols to determine which chemicals, drugs and foodstuffs are safe and which dangerous and in what amounts; an unlimited supply of animal organs for human transplant with no problems of rejection; animals that can act as 'drug factories,' churning out huge amounts of effective drugs in their milk. . . .

Inappropriate Models for Toxicology Testing

In recent years, transgenesis [the insertion of foreign genetic coding into an animal] has been used in what can only be considered to be a last-ditch attempt to derive some form of useful information from animals used in toxicity testing. For decades, the assessment of which chemicals, drugs, food additives and so on might pose a hazard to human health has relied heavily upon administering them to mice and rats, and examining their tissues for damage. It is now universally accepted that the correlation between results from these investigations are in the region of 5–30%, a statistic that belies claims that these tests can be in any way predictive of human response.

The FDA Deputy Commissioner Discusses the Risks of GM Animals Used for Food

The Food and Drug Administration is familiar with the risks of biotechnology. We are aware that using genetically altered animals for food raises serious safety concerns that must be addressed through rigorous, science-based analysis. Bioactive compounds are a good example. They include growth hormones, proteins that aid in resisting disease, and even proteins of pharmaceutical interest. If these proteins are present in edible tissues of transgenic animals, they might pose a food safety risk.

Allergic reactions are another concern. The risk of adverse reactions is raised whenever foods contain new proteins from genetically modified organisms, regardless of whether their source is an animal, plant, or microorganism such as yeast or bacteria.

Lester Crawford, "Genetic Kingdom:
Reaping the Bounties of Our Biotech Future,"
American Enterprise, *vol. 15, no. 2, March 2004.*

And so these mice have been transformed into new, improved transgenic animals that are now more susceptible to the harmful effects of various substances—and, it is hoped, be more predictive of which substances will poison and/or cause cancer in human beings. The reality is that transgenic animals are continuing to produce inconsistent results and be of no predictive value in such assessments, and that no single transgenic animal or combination of transgenic animals performs nearly well enough to be considered sufficiently reliable for regulatory use. For example, genetically engineered mice manipulated to investigate genes involved in cancers of the nervous system in children showed that some genes and mutations clearly associated with specific human tumours produced very different effects in mice, and that one cancer-causing genetic pathway in rats did not operate in any human tumours. . . .

The Unknown Dangers of Pharming

Human proteins are used therapeutically in the treatment of a wide range of diseases, such as multiple sclerosis, hepatitis, cancer, cystic fibrosis and malaria. These proteins have been successfully produced via a number of methods for some years, including GM [genetically modified] bacterial and yeast cultures, cultures of mammalian and plant cells, and entire GM plant crops, with each method having distinct advantages and disadvantages. Transgenic animals have been added to this list more recently, not due to necessity, but mainly because companies producing the therapeutic proteins believe that, once developed, pharmaceutical-producing GM animals can be scaled up to a huge degree and will then generate almost limitless amounts of product very cheaply.

Cows, chickens, goats, pigs, rabbits and sheep have been genetically engineered to produce therapeutic proteins in an industry known as 'pharming' or 'biopharming.' The animals are manipulated so that they produce these products in their milk, mostly, but also in their urine, blood, or even sperm. Large amounts of these proteins are then purified and processed into a final product. . . . There are some . . . problems specific to pharming. In principle, transgene expression is intended to be confined to, for example, the mammary gland in those animals engineered to produce the transgene protein product in their milk. However, 'leaky' gene expression is often detected in other tissues, and the proteins are often found in the animals' blood. This can have severe negative health consequences, causing animals to suffer from 'pathologies and other severe systemic effects', as reported by the National Academy of Sciences in the USA.

Scientific and medical concerns surrounding these endeavours include, in common with xenotransplantation, the risk of cross-species disease transmission. This risk, of course, is real, though it may be considered minor by patients relying upon a transgenic therapeutic protein to ameliorate their suffering and/or disease. In addition, it is a statement of fact that many if not most human proteins will not be 'as they should' structurally, functionally and biochemically unless they are produced in a human milieu, i.e. in cultured human cells. Some proteins are absolutely fine being produced in bacteria, for example, but others show marked differences—ranging from ostensibly inconsequential, superficial changes, to massive and catastrophic ones. Proteins in the latter class need to be produced in 'higher' cells . . . so why produce them in cow's milk instead of cultured human cells? The only answer is: profit. And to produce such therapeutic proteins in transgenic animals, with all that the process entails, when this is not strictly necessary, can be regarded as ethically abhorrent and unjustifiable, especially in cases where they could be efficiently produced using plants and other means.

| "Animal cloning . . . was initiated to seek
fundamental knowledge for the benefit
of humankind."

Animal Cloning Is Worthwhile

Marie A. Di Berardino

In the following viewpoint Marie A. Di Berardino describes the process of cloning animals and asserts that this practice promises benefits to medicine and agriculture. As Berardino explains, biotechnology has already shown, for example, how genetically modified animals can produce beneficial human proteins. Cloning these animals, in her opinion, could create whole herds of protein producers. She also attests that cloning genetically enhanced livestock could similarly improve reproduction rates, meat quality, and milk production for the agriculture industry. Marie A. Di Berardino is a professor emerita of biochemistry at the Medical College of Pennsylvania-Hahnemann University in Philadelphia.

As you read, consider the following questions:

1. What is Polly and why is she significant, in the author's view?

Marie A. Di Berardino, "Cloning: Past, Present, and the Exciting Future," *Breakthroughs in Bioscience*, Federation of American Societies for Experimental Biology, n.d., pp. 1–8. www.faseb.org. Reproduced by permission.

2. As Di Berardino states, how can cloned animals be help-ful to xenotransplantation?

3. How is nuclear transfer technology being used to inves-tigate the aging process, according to Di Berardino?

Jimmy walks into the neighborhood pharmacy to fill his prescription for a protein he was born without. He lacks the gene for blood clotting factor IX and relies on the local drug-store for his medicine. Jimmy pulls open the bag that contains his 90-day supply of patches, removes the old patch from his chest, and attaches a new one. He adjusts his jersey and heads out to meet his buddies for a game of touch football. Even though he is hemophiliac, Jimmy isn't worried about the bruises and scrapes he is sure to get. . . .

This is the future. It is what Dolly so wondrously has wrought. Born July 1996, she is the first mammal successfully cloned from an adult cell, one taken from a ewe's mammary gland.

The Nuclear Transfer Process

Dolly was not created in the ordinary way. Typically, a lamb is the product of natural reproduction—two germ cells, a sperm from an adult male and an egg (oocyte) from an adult female, fuse at fertilization. Each of these germ cells (the sperm and the oocyte) contributes half the chromosomes needed to cre-ate a new individual. Chromosomes are found in the cell's nucleus and they carry the DNA, which is the genetic blue-print for an individual.

The process that produced Dolly differs from ordinary re-production in two major ways. First, body (or somatic) cells from an adult ewe's udder (this is the donor) were placed in a culture dish and allowed to grow. The nutrients were then re-moved from the culture, which stopped the cells' growth. One of these non-growing cells was then fused (by electric jolts) with another ewe's oocyte from which the nucleus had been previously removed (i.e., enucleated, so it had no chromosomes). This procedure is known as 'somatic cell nuclear transfer'. Within a day the fused cells began to divide in the culture dish. After several divisions, the early embryo was transferred to the uterus of a surrogate mother and allowed to develop.

Second, unlike the sperm and the egg, each of which contributes half the number of chromosomes at fertilization, each body cell contains twice the number of chromosomes in each germ cell. So fusion of a sperm and an egg forms an individual whose full genetic composition is unique to that individual. On the other hand, the embryo cloned from somatic cell nuclear transfer begins development with the diploid (double) number of chromosomes, all derived from one somatic cell (adult udder) of a single individual. This embryo has the same nuclear genetic composition as the donor of the somatic cell. . . .

Transgenic Protein Producers

Imagine herds of female sheep, cattle, and goats producing large quantities of human proteins in their milk, an ideal place for those proteins to be harvested and used to treat patients like Jimmy, the hemophiliac, whose blood cannot clot. We can realize this dream today—one step at a time, because the process that produced Dolly also can be used to produce the transgenic (one species carrying another species' genes) clones.

Scottish scientists first removed cells from a fetal lamb and grew them in a culture dish. Multiple copies of fragments of DNA (deoxyribonucleic acid, which holds genetic information) containing the human gene for blood clotting factor IX were added to the dish and coaxed into the cells. Some cells incorporated the human DNA into their chromosomes, thus becoming 'transgenic cells', or cells containing a transferred gene.

These transgenic cells were then separated from those without human DNA and used to create Polly, the transgenic sheep that today produces the human clotting factor IX in her milk. Purposely, scientists genetically designed the transgenic sheep clones so that the human gene would function only in the mammary gland.

It will soon be possible for the human clotting factor IX protein to be routinely harvested and purified from the sheep milk. . . .

The importance of the transgenic clones is that biotechnology is now being extended to produce different human proteins like insulin (diabetes), interferon (viral infections), clotting factor VIII (hemophilia), and tissue plasminogen activator (dissolving blood clots). In other words, female clones of such animals as cattle, sheep, and goats are being genetically designed to be dairy/pharmaceutical producers, a virtual living bio-pharmaceutical industry. Transgenic clones of mammals are a major advance in biotechnology because they can synthesize, in large quantities, complex molecules critically required for patient care. . . .

Other Benefits of Clones

While these advances are on the horizon for us, beneficial applications to agriculture are already being implemented. Transgenic cloning can be used for the genetic improvement of livestock related to milk production, quality of meat, growth rate, reproduction, nutrition, behavioral traits, and/or resistance to diseases. This cloning process simply accelerates the older, slower, and less predictable methods of crossbreeding and hybridization. . . .

Transgenic clones can be directly beneficial to humans, other animals, and agriculture in additional ways.

- They may be developed for tissue and organ transplantation. Although not yet a reality, there is promise that large animals can be genetically designed and cloned so

Sexual reproduction (A) and somatic cell nuclear transfer (B) in sheep

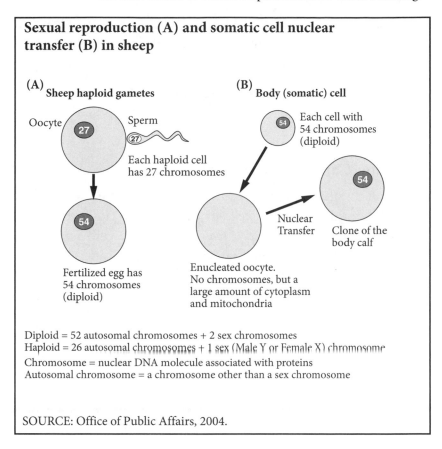

Diploid = 52 autosomal chromosomes + 2 sex chromosomes
Haploid = 26 autosomal chromosomes + 1 sex (Male Y or Female X) chromosome
Chromosome = nuclear DNA molecule associated with proteins
Autosomal chromosome = a chromosome other than a sex chromosome

SOURCE: Office of Public Affairs, 2004.

that their tissues and organs will not trigger immunological responses in the recipient and cause them to be rejected. Recently, muscle rigidity and tremors in parkinsonian rats were improved by transplanting cloned transgenic bovine neurons into their brains. This research, called xenotransplantation, is one of the many avenues being pursued in an attempt to alleviate the desperate shortage of human tissues for transplantation.

• Domestic animals can be genetically designed to express a certain human disease and therefore serve as models for the study and treatment of human illnesses. Although many mouse models of human diseases are available today, such models in large domestic animals physiologically more similar to humans are sparse and critically needed.

- Somatic cell nuclear transfer might help preserve endangered species such as pandas that have low reproductive rates.

Fighting Cancer and the Aging Process

Two other significant gains from clones are worth mentioning.

First, inducing cancer cells to differentiate [to mature into a specific cell type, such as a liver cell or skin cell] is a useful type of therapy. We know that many types of cancer cells are less specialized than their normal counterparts. For this reason investigators suspected that the precursors of cancer cells could be immature cells or stem cells that fail to complete differentiation. If this is so, then by using information gained from nuclear transfer technology, we may be able to induce the cells to mature and stop making tumors. Previous studies have demonstrated that we can control at least some cancer cells by using the differentiation process.

Second, aged cell nuclei can be rejuvenated. People and other organisms change as they age. Environmental insults and diseases cause these changes; others are intrinsic to the organism. Studies using cell culture have shown that body cells grow and divide normally in culture for awhile, but eventually stop dividing, become senescent [become aged and lose the ability to divide and replicate], and die. An exception was seen in aged frog red blood cell nuclei (human red blood cells lack nuclei): After their transfer into enucleated oocytes, frog red blood cell nuclei were rejuvenated. They carried out the formation of tadpoles that survived almost a third of the way to metamorphosis. The oocyte cytoplasm contains an abundance of chemicals that promote DNA synthesis and cell division after normal fertilization. We believe that these substances also rejuvenate aged cell nuclei and turn non-cycling frog red blood cells into active ones. If we could isolate these substances, we might be able to alleviate—or reverse—senescence. . . .

Ethical Choices

The choices we make for the application of knowledge reside in ethical decisions by humans. Animal cloning, like other research, was initiated to seek fundamental knowledge for the benefit of humankind. In addition to expanding the knowledge base in cellular, developmental, and molecular biology, as well as in cancer and aging, cloning has now been applied to enhance medicine and agriculture. Presently, hospital committees in the United States bar attempts to clone humans because of clinical, safety, and ethical concerns. Cloning is only one of many discoveries in which society will have to choose which applications are ethical and which ones are not.

> *"Like pet cloning, the cloning of farm animals is monumentally unnecessary."*

Animal Cloning Is Unnecessary

Wayne Pacelle

Wayne Pacelle is the president of the Humane Society of the United States. In the following viewpoint Pacelle argues that animal cloning is an unneeded technological advance. According to Pacelle, the cloning of pets or farm livestock is unnecessary because there is no current shortage of these animals. Pet owners who want to clone their deceased animals are merely acting out of vanity, Pacelle maintains, while the cloning of livestock is motivated purely by profit. Before this technology moves forward, Pacelle urges that policy makers consider the risks to both humans and animals.

As you read, consider the following questions:

1. What are two of the reasons why Pacelle objects to pet cloning?
2. What impact does Pacelle predict agricultural animal cloning will have on small farmers?

3. According to the author, what animal welfare concerns are raised by animal cloning?

With the arrival of Little Nicky, a kitten cloned to duplicate a Dallas woman's deceased pet, animal cloning has moved from closed-door laboratories to commercial application. The $50,000 feline was delivered by Genetic Savings & Clone, the playfully named company catering to particularly devoted pet owners.

While the intentions of the pet owners are understandable, the practice itself is rife with hazard and requires a decisive response from policy-makers. There are many practical problems with pet cloning, not the least of which is that the genetic duplicate may turn out to act, and even look, different from its forebear. Each creature—shaped in part by life experience—is more than an embodiment of his or her DNA. A cloned animal may look much the same and bring back happy memories for pet lovers, but the creature they are looking at is not the same animal.

More to the point, with millions of healthy and adoptable cats and dogs being killed each year for lack of suitable homes, it's a little frivolous to be cloning departed pets. The challenge is not to find new, absurdly expensive ways to create animals, but to curb the growth of pet populations and to foster an ethic in society that prompts people to adopt and shelter creatures in need of loving homes.

Untold Risks Need Reassessment

Pet cloning is simply not worth repeating. Behind this one little kitten are far grander schemes to clone animals for use in agriculture and research. Before such projects become the norm, we should pause and think carefully about where it is leading—for animals and for humanity.

It was big news some years ago when scientists in Scotland announced the cloning of Dolly the sheep. This new technology marked a decisive moment in our ability to manipulate the natural world to suit our designs. Dolly has long since passed afflicted by a lung disease that typically occurs in much older sheep. Since her dramatic birth—and her pitiful decline—scientists have turned out clones for mice, rabbits, goats, pigs, cows and now cats. Cloned horses and dogs, we are promised, are on the way. But behind every heralded success are hundreds of monstrous failures.

As all of this has unfolded, policy-makers have stood idly by, failing to place any restraints of law and ethics on corporations and scientists who are tinkering here with the most fundamental elements of biology. We hear indignation and expressions of well-founded concern about human cloning. But we hear hardly a word of doubt or moral concern about the idea of animal cloning, much less about the particular animals subjected to these experiments. It won't be long before biotech companies in the hire of agribusiness announce plans to sell commercial clones as food. Cloned ham, steak, and even drumsticks may be served at retail operations in the future, and there's no law to forbid the sale of meat or milk from clones produced in a laboratory.

Like pet cloning, the cloning of farm animals is monumentally unnecessary. Farmers are already producing so much meat that they must find export markets to turn a profit. As for milk, it's cheaper than bottled water. The dairy industry recently "culled" tens of thousands of healthy dairy cows in order to depress production.

Small farmers, already put at a disadvantage by mounting debt and mechanized competitors, will be further marginalized as cloning practices become commonplace. More than ever, they'll be at the mercy of corporate factory farms to purchase their supply of clones.

Consumers face threats of a different sort. Who knows if consuming meat and milk from clones is safe? A recent Food and Drug Administration symposium addressed this issue, but

Sutton. © by Ward Sutton. Reproduced by permission.

the confident declarations that the animal products are safe didn't seem all that reassuring: Just one misstep could be catastrophic. With mad cow, foot-and-mouth, avian flu and other diseases now posing a greater threat in our globalized agricultural markets, the production of genetically identical animals would pose serious threats to food security. Genetic variation, already low from conventional breeding, would also be almost eliminated by cloning.

Animal Welfare Concerns

As for the animals in our factory farms, cloning is the final assault on their well-being and dignity. When the FDA held a public consultation on animal cloning in November 2003, researchers reported a graphic list of problems for clones and their surrogate mothers in cattle, pigs, sheep and goats—a string of developmental abnormalities and a host of deaths before, during and after birth. The animals being cloned exhibit grievous problems, such as cows with grossly enlarged udders, major leg problems and other forms of lameness. And these are the very animals trumpeted as success stories.

Of the largest group of clones yet—produced by Cyagra, which clones cattle—few embryos survived to term, and of those that did, a third then died by the age of 1 year. The FDA's report, "Animal Cloning: A Risk Assessment" put a nice spin on this when it said that "the proportion of live, normal births appears to be increasing." In other words, the situation has improved from atrocious to very bad.

It is time for Congress and the FDA and other regulatory bodies to engage in the animal-cloning debate. Many of the ethical concerns raised by human cloning apply to this reckless disregard for the integrity of animal life. Should such questions be left entirely to scientists and corporations, since they have an intellectual and commercial stake in these projects? Our government alone can stand up for the public interest in preventing this cruelty.

Cloning is a startling procedure, to be sure, and many scientists would have us view it as some inevitable stage in our technological development. But humanity's progress is not always defined by scientific innovation alone. Cloning—both human and animal—is one of those cases in which progress is defined by the exercise of wisdom and of self-restraint.

Periodical Bibliography

The following articles have been selected to supplement the diverse views presented in this chapter.

Roy Calne	"Xenografting—The Future of Transplantation, and Always Will Be," *Xenotransptantation*, 2005.
Philip Cohen and David Concar	"The Awful Truth: Cloning of Prize Animals Is Already Economic," *New Scientist*, May 19, 2001.
David K.C. Cooper	"Clinical Xenotransplantion—How Close Are We?" *Lancet*, August 16, 2003.
Simon Cooper	"The Small Matter of Our Humanity," *Arena*, June–July 2002.
Lester Crawford	"Reaping the Biotech Harvest," *Biotech Bounty*, March 2004.
Anthony Dorling	"Clinical Xenotransplantation. Pigs Might Fly!" *American Journal of Xenotransplantation*, 2002.
Economist	"Down on the Pharm," September 18, 2004.
Alix Fano	"One Man's Meat: Transplanting Organs from Pigs and Monkeys to Humans," *Ecologist*, December 2000.
Tony Gill	"The Atomic Fish: The Rising Controversy of Genetically Modified Pets," *Humanist*, September–October 2004.
Cheryl V. Hunter, Laurence S. Tiley, and Helen M. Sang	"Developments in Transgenic Technology: Applications for Medicine," *Trends in Molecular Medicine*, June 2005.
A. Ravelingien and J. Braeckman	"To the Core of Porcine Matter: Evaluating Arguments Against Producing Transgenic Pigs," *Xenotransplantation*, 2004.
Arlene Weintraub	"Crossing the Gene Barrier," *Business Week*, January 16, 2006.

For Further Discussion

Chapter 1

1. Ilana Mercer argues that animals cannot have rights because they act without conscience. In her opinion, only humans can derive rights because of their "innate moral agency and capacity for reason." Tom Regan, on the other hand, claims that humans should recognize and respect the inherent rights of animals because it is the "just" thing to do—and "justice is the highest principle of ethics." After examining these two views, decide how each author defines the source of rights. Do you think animals have inherent rights or are people the only creatures that can claim to have rights? Explain your answers while referencing the arguments given by the authors.

2. Matt Ball and Jack Norris question the notion that animals cannot possess rights equal to humans because they are simply not human. They point out, for example, that not all humans share the same rights, and therefore the matter of being human cannot be the sole deciding factor of who or what deserves rights. Ball and Norris suggest that the capacity to suffer should be the measure of whom or what can claim to possess rights. Josie Appleton, however, argues that while animals and humans both suffer, the distinction between humans and animal species has more to do with consciousness. Explain how Appleton argues her case that animals cannot attain rights because they are fundamentally different than humans. In the end, decide whether you support Ball and Norris's claim that rights belong to all creatures because humans are not of demonstrably superior value, or whether you believe Appleton's assertion that rights are apportioned by kind, not degree. Defend your answer.

3. Alex Epstein and Will Potter have opposing opinions on whether the actions of animal rights activists constitute terrorism. Epstein maintains that extremists' actions often tend toward terrorism, Potter suggests that activists' actions are often unfairly labeled as terrorism. After examining the authors' views, do you believe there are some grounds on which Epstein and Potter may agree? What are they? In your opinion, has either author been too harsh or too lenient in judging the actions of animal activists? Use examples from the viewpoints, as well as any other reported incidents involving animal activists, to support your answer.

Chapter 2

1. Adrian R. Morrison contends that it is moral to use animals in medical research because it is the duty of humans to keep their own race alive—in the same way that all species fight to continue their existence. David Thomas, on the other hand, believes that it is immoral to conduct experiments on any unwilling creature—animal or human—because the potential to cause pain and suffering forms the basis for all ethical judgments. Which author do you believe presents the strongest argument concerning the morality or immorality of animal experimentation? Do you think that either author has correctly identified the basis of human morality? If not, what other fundamentals of morality, in your view, impact the animal experimentation debate?

2. After examining the arguments of John Gray and the Scientific Steering Committee of the European Commission, how do you feel about the use of nonhuman primates in animal experimentation? Should research continue because apes are such excellent models for studying human diseases, or is their similarity to humans a reason to abolish nonhuman primate experiments? Explain your answer.

3. Considering the arguments made in all the viewpoints in this chapter, do you think there is a way for the competing camps to compromise on animal experimentation? That is, like the system proposed by Patrick Bateson, could there be a method to determine when animal experiments should be tolerated and when they should not? What would be your criteria for making such a judgment? In framing your answer, consider your opinion of the value and sentience of all life. Is conducting experiments on earthworms, for example, the same as conducting them on chimpanzees?

Chapter 3

1. The American Physiological Society (APS) cites several areas of research in which animal experimentation has aided medical progress. Christopher Anderegg and his colleagues list other examples in which animal experimentation has hindered or had no impact on medical advances. Which set of authors do you think wages a more convincing argument with its examples? The APS also gives several reasons why animals make excellent test subjects, while Anderegg provides many limitations of animal models. Which side makes the more persuasive argument regarding this issue? Explain your answers when responding to both questions.

2. Consider the arguments presented in the viewpoints of Kathy Archibald and David H. Freedman. Do you think that alternatives to animal drug testing are or will ever be as accurate as animal models? Explain why or why not.

Chapter 4

1. Joyce D'Silva argues that animal-to-human transplantation is too risky to implement because of unknown factors that include the possibility of widespread disease transmission. Conversely, the unnamed physician interviewed by Gale

Scott claims that xenotransplantation is too attractive an option not to pursue because it will ensure better and cheaper transplant organs than are available from human donors. Considering that tens of thousands of people waiting for transplants each year do not receive needed organs, do you think it is more appropriate to speed xenotransplantation or to restrict its implementation? Do you think that policies should be changed so that patients could take the responsibility for accepting animal organs regardless of the unknown consequences? Explain why or why not.

2. The viewpoints by Alexandre Fouassier, *Manufacturing Chemist*, Animal Aid, Marie A. Di Berardino, and Wayne Pacelle all contend with the pros and cons, rights and wrongs of manipulating animal genetics to aid humans. Fouassier and Di Berardino argue, for example, that creating transgenic livestock that can produce human proteins will help human patients in need of these proteins. Animal Aid and Wayne Pacelle counter that other methods are available to produce such proteins and that the creation of cloned herds of genetically modified animals is unnecessary and motivated solely by profits. Which argument do you find more persuasive? Explain why.

3. Wayne Pacelle notes a connection between the ethical issues surrounding animal cloning and those surrounding human cloning. Many who speak out against animal cloning, in fact, argue that to condone it would bring humanity one step closer to tolerating human cloning. Do you think animal cloning paves the way to human cloning, or is there a distinction (moral or otherwise) that separates the issues? In your opinion, should all cloning be condemned or condoned, or should animal cloning be tolerated while human cloning remains banned? Explain your decision while referencing some of the arguments made in this chapter.

Organizations to Contact

The editors have compiled the following list of organizations concerned with the issues debated in this book. The descriptions are derived from materials provided by the organizations. All have publications or information available for interested readers. The list was compiled on the date of publication of the present volume; the information provided here may change. Be aware that many organizations take several weeks or longer to respond to inquiries, so allow as much time as possible.

Advanced Cell Technology (ACT)
1201 Harbor Bay Pkwy., Suite 120, Alameda, CA   94502
(510) 748-4900 • fax: (510) 748-4950
Web site: www.advancedcell.com

The first to successfully clone an endangered animal by duplicating its cells and implanting them into another species, ACT also engages in animal cloning for technology development and drug screening. Its Web site contains links to reports and press releases that are published in various scientific magazines, as well as to testimonials, letters, and reports regarding the ethical issues of cloning.

American Anti-Vivisection Society (AAVS)
801 Old York Rd., Suite 204, Jenkintown, PA   19046
(800) 729-2287
e-mail: aavs@aavs.org
Web site: www.aavs.org

AAVS advocates the abolition of vivisection, opposes all types of experiments on living animals, and sponsors research on alternatives to these methods. The society produces videos and publishes numerous brochures, including *Dissection and Students' Rights*, as well as the award-winning *AV Magazine*.

American Association for Laboratory Animal Science (AALAS)

9190 Crestwyn Hills Dr., Memphis, TN   38125
(901) 754-8620 • fax: (901) 759-5849
e-mail: info@aalas.org
Web site: www.aalas.org

The American Association for Laboratory Animal Science is a professional nonprofit association of persons and institutions concerned with the production, care, and study of animals used in biomedical research. This organization provides a medium for the exchange of scientific information on all phases of laboratory animal care and use through its educational activities, publications, and certification program. Its publications include *Contemporary Topics in Laboratory Animal Science* and *Laboratory Animal Science.*

Americans for Medical Progress (AMP)

908 King St., Suite 301, Alexandria, VA   22314
(703) 836-9595 • fax: (703) 836-9594
e-mail: info@amprogress.org
Web site: www.amprogress.org

AMP is a nonprofit organization that raises public awareness concerning the use of animals in research. Its goal is to ensure that scientists and doctors have the freedom and resources necessary to pursue their work. To that end, AMP exposes the misinformation of the animal rights movement through newspaper and magazine articles, broadcast debates, and public education materials.

Animal Aid

The Old Chapel, Bradford St.
Tonbridge, Kent, TN9 1AW   United Kingdom
(44) 73 236 4546 • fax: 44 (0) 73 236 6533
e-mail: info@animalaid.org.uk
Web site: www.animalaid.org.uk

Animal Aid investigates and exposes animal cruelty. The organization stages street protests and education tours. It also publishes educational packets for schools and colleges.

Animal Alliance of Canada
221 Broadview Avenue, Suite 101
Toronto, ON   M4M 2G3   Canada
(416) 462-9541 • fax: (416) 462-9647
e-mail: info@animalalliance.ca
Web site: www.animalalliance.ca

The Animal Alliance of Canada is an animal rights advocacy and education group that focuses on local, regional, national, and international issues concerning the respectful treatment of animals by humans. Animal Alliance acts through research, investigation, education, advocacy, and legislation. Publications include fact sheets, legislative updates, editorials, and the newsletter *Take Action.*

Animal Liberation Front (ALF)
21044 Sherman Way, #211, Canoga Park, CA   91302
(818) 932-9997 • fax: (818) 932-9998
e-mail: press@animalliberationpressoffice.org
Web site: www.animalliberationfront.com

ALF seeks to end worldwide animal exploitation and otherwise reduce the suffering of animals. The organization's Web site contains information on how to take action against institutionalized animal exploitation. The site also archives personal stories of animal activism, opinion articles, interviews, and profiles of noted activists. Educational materials on vivisection, animal experimentation, and toxicity testing are also available to download.

Animal Welfare Institute (AWI)
PO Box 3650, Washington, DC   20007
(703) 836-4300 • fax: (703) 836-0400
e-mail: awi@animalwelfare.org
Web site: www.awionline.org

AWI is a nonprofit charitable organization working to reduce pain and fear inflicted on animals by humans. It advocates the humane treatment of laboratory animals and the development and use of nonanimal testing methods. AWI encourages humane science teaching and the prevention of painful experiments on animals in the classroom. In addition to publishing *AWI Quarterly*, the institute also offers numerous books, pamphlets, and online articles.

Foundation for Biomedical Research (FBR)

818 Connecticut Ave. NW, Suite 900, Washington, DC   20006
(202) 457-0654 • fax: (202) 457-0659
e-mail: info@fbresearch.org
Web site: www.fbresearch.org

FBR is the oldest organization in the United States dedicated to promoting animal research in the pursuit of improving human and animal health. It therefore opposes animal activists who try to thwart the use of animals in biomedical research. The organization's Web site contains press releases and fact sheets on the value of animal research.

Fund for Animals

200 West 57th St., New York, NY   10019
(888) 405-3863
Web site: www.fundforanimals.org

The Fund for Animals was founded in 1967 by prominent author and animal advocate Cleveland Amory. It remains one of the largest and most active organizations working for the welfare of both wild and domesticated animals throughout the world. The fund promotes its message through education, lobbying, and litigation.

In Defense of Animals

3010 Kerner Blvd., San Rafael, CA   94901
(415) 388-9641 • fax: (415) 388-0388
e-mail: ida@idausa.org
Web site: www.idausa.org

In Defense of Animals is a nonprofit organization established in 1983 that works to end the institutional exploitation and abuse of laboratory animals. The organization publishes fact sheets and brochures on animal abuse in the laboratory and how to live a cruelty-free lifestyle.

Institute for In Vitro Sciences (IIVS)
21 Firstfield Rd., Suite 220, Gaithersburg, MD   20878
(301) 947-6523 • fax: (301) 947-6538
Web site: www.iivs.org

IIVS is a nonprofit, technology-driven foundation for the advancement of alternative methods to animal testing. Its mission is to facilitate the replacement of animal testing through the use of in vitro technology. IIVS provides educational and technical resources available to corporate, government, and public interests. It also makes its published articles available on its Web site.

Medical Research Modernization Committee (MRMC)
3200 Morley Rd., Shaker Heights, OH   44122
(216) 283-6702
Web site: www.mrmcmed.org

MRMC is a national health advocacy group composed of physicians, scientists, and other health care professionals who evaluate the benefits, risks, and costs of medical research methods and technologies. The committee believes that animals are inadequate models for testing medical treatments and that research money would be better spent on human clinical trials.

National Animal Interest Alliance (NAIA)
PO Box 66579, Portland, OR   97290
(503) 761-1139
e-mail: naia@naiaonline.org
Web site: www.naiaonline.org

NAIA is an association of business, agricultural, scientific, and recreational interests formed to protect and promote humane practices and relationships between people and animals. NAIA provides the network necessary for diverse animal rights groups to communicate with one another, to describe the nature and value of their work, to clarify animal rights misinformation, and to educate each other and the public about what they do. NAIA serves as a clearinghouse for information; it also publishes the bimonthly newspaper *NAIA News*.

Patients' Voice for Medical Advance
PO Box 504, Dunstable, Bedfordshire LUS 5WS
United Kingdom
(44) 58 286 7766 • fax: (44) 58 286 7766
e-mail: info@patientsvoice.org.uk
Web site: www.patientsvoice.org.uk

Patient's Voice for Medical Advance is a patients' group formed to voice support for humane research into disabling, incurable, and progressive diseases. The organization promotes the following objectives: a greater public understanding of the methods, aims, and benefits of animal research; the provision of the resources necessary for medical research to be conducted; and appropriate legislation relating to medicine and medical research. The group publishes the *Hope* newsletter.

People for the Ethical Treatment of Animals (PETA)
501 Front St., Norfolk, VA   23510
(757) 622-7382 • fax: (757) 622-0457
e-mail: peta@norfolk.infini.net
Web site: www.peta.org

An international animal rights organization, PETA is dedicated to establishing and protecting the rights of animals. It focuses on four areas: factory farms, research laboratories, the fur trade, and the entertainment industry. PETA promotes public education, cruelty investigations, animal rescue, celebrity involvement, and legislative and direct action. It produces numerous videos and publishes *Animal Times*, various fact sheets, brochures, and flyers.

Physicians Committee for Responsible Medicine (PCRM)
5100 Wisconsin Ave. NW, Suite 400, Washington, DC   20016
(202) 686-2210
e-mail: pcrm@pcrm.org
Web site: www.pcrm.org

Founded in 1985, PCRM is a nonprofit organization supported by physicians and laypersons that encourages higher standards for ethics and effectiveness in research. PCRM promotes using animal alternatives in both research and education. The committee publishes the quarterly magazine *Good Medicine* and numerous fact sheets on animal experimentation issues.

Uncaged Campaigns
9 Bailey Lane, Sheffield   S1 4EG
UK
(44) 14 272 2220 • fax: (44) 14 272 2225
e-mail: info@uncaged.co.uk
Web site: www.uncaged.co.uk

Uncaged Campaigns works to end vivisection and to ascribe moral and legal rights to animals. It stages demonstrations as well as lobbies for legislative change. The organization's Web site contains fact sheets and an archive of news articles.

Bibliography of Books

Diane L. Beers *For the Prevention of Cruelty: The History and Legacy of Animal Rights Activism in the United States.* Athens, OH: Swallow, 2006.

Ruth Ellen Bulger et al. *The Ethical Dimensions of the Biological and Health Sciences.* New York: Cambridge University Press, 2002.

Peter Carruthers *The Animals Issue: Moral Theory in Practice.* New York: Cambridge University Press, 1992.

Carl Cohen and Tom Regan *The Animal Rights Debate.* Lanham, MD: Rowman & Littlefield, 2001.

David K.C. Cooper and Robert P. Lanza *XENO: The Promise of Transplanting Animal Organs into Humans.* New York: Oxford University Press, 2000.

Pietro Croce *Vivisection or Science?: An Investigation into Testing Drugs and Safeguarding Health.* New York: Zed, 1999.

Alix Fano *Lethal Laws: Animal Testing, Human Health and Environmental Policy.* New York: St. Martin's, 1998.

Lawrence Finsen and Susan Finsen *The Animal Rights Movement in America: From Compassion to Respect.* New York: Twayne, 1994.

Michael Allen Fox   *The Case for Animal Experimentation: An Evolutionary and Ethical Perspective.* Berkeley: University of California Press, 1986.

Julian H. Franklin   *Animal Rights and Moral Philosophy.* New York: Columbia University Press, 2005.

Temple Grandin and Catherine Johnson   *Animals in Translation: Using the Mysteries of Autism to Decode Animal Behavior.* San Diego: Harvest, 2005.

C. Ray Greek and Jean Swingle Greek   *Sacred Cows and Golden Geese: The Human Cost of Experiments with Animals.* New York: Continuum, 2000.

Anita Guerrini   *Experimenting with Humans and Animals: From Galen to Animal Rights.* Baltimore: Johns Hopkins University Press, 2003.

Harold D. Guither   *Animal Rights: History and Scope of a Radical Social Movement.* Carbondale: Southern Illinois University Press, 1998.

Andrew Linzey and Paul Barry Clarke, eds.   *Animal Rights: A Historical Anthology.* New York: Columbia University Press, 2004.

Mary Midgley   *Animals and Why They Matter.* Athens: University of Georgia Press, 1983.

Ingrid Newkirk   *Save the Animals.* New York: Warner Books, 1990.

Martha C. Nussbaum — *Frontiers of Justice: Disability, Nationality, Species Membership.* Cambridge, MA: Belknap, 2006.

Barbara Orlans — *In the Name of Science: Issues in Responsible Animal Experimentation.* New York: Oxford University Press, 1993.

Tony Page — *Vivisection Unveiled: An Exposé of the Medical Futility of Animal Experimentation.* Oxford, UK: Jon Carpenter, 1998.

Ellen Frankel Paul and Jeffrey Paul, eds. — *Why Animal Experimentation Matters: The Use of Animals in Medical Research.* New Brunswick, NJ: Transaction, 2001.

Tom Regan — *Empty Cages: Facing the Challenge of Animal Rights.* Lanham, MD: Rowman & Littlefield, 2004.

Mark Rowlands — *Animals Like Us.* London, UK: Verso, 2002.

Peter Singer — *Animal Liberation.* New York: Random House, 1990.

Peter Singer, ed. — *In Defense of Animals: The Second Wave.* Malden, MA: Blackwell, 2006.

Richard Sorabji — *Animal Minds and Human Morals: The Origins of the Western Debate.* Ithaca, NY: Cornell University Press, 1993.

Cass Sunstein and Martha Nussbaum	*Animal Rights: Current Debates and New Directions.* New York: Oxford University Press, 2004.
Donna Yarri	The *Ethics of Animal Experimentation: A Critical Analysis and Constructive Christian Proposal.* New York: Oxford University Press, 2005.

Index

Abrikosov, Alexei A., 31–32

aging process, 202–203

agriculture, transgenic clones used for, 200

AIDS research
animal-based research is needed for, 153–54
animal models prove useless for, 149
primates used for, 105, 115, 147

American Association for Laboratory Animal Science, 156

American Physiological Society, 138

ancient Egypt, 46

ancient Greece, 46–47

Anderegg, Christopher, 144

Animal Aid, 192

Animal Enterprise Protection Act (1992), 17

Animal Enterprise Terrorism Act (1992), 60, 63

Animal Liberation (group), 22

Animal Liberation (Singer), 45

Animal Procedures Committee (APC), 85, 89

animal research
certainty of benefits from, 129–31
finding replacements for, 127–28
U.S. statistics on, 122
see also animal research debate; biomedical research

animal research community
British government is on side of, 85
conflicting ethical views with animal rights activists, 119–20
effectiveness of activism against, 61

guinea pigs raised for, 14
is silenced by animal rights activists, 65–67
on limiting animal experimentation, 130
must end deadlock over animal research debate, 122–23
past view by, 127
questioning motives of, 126–27
should speak out about animal research, 67–68
see also Huntingdon Life Sciences (HLS)

animal research debate, 17–18
conflicting ethical views and, 119–20
deadlock over, 119
scientific community must make next move to end, 122–23
decision rules for reconciling, 131–33
intensity of, 125
making difficult decisions and, 129–31
reconciling different moral positions and, 129
use of violence and, 121–22

animal research, ethics and justification of
ability to exercise responsibility and, 79, 93
based on intelligence, problems with, 92–93
because animals are not little persons, 78
because of our obligation to humans, 75–76
because of the drive to survive, 74–75
conflicting views on, 119–20
deontological approach to, 98, 100

experiments on people are comparable to, 90–91

issue of consent and, 94–98

issue of suffering and, 100–101

in primates
con, 110–17
pro, 103–109

problem with hierarchies of value and, 91–92

rational thought and, 86–87

secrecy of system, and ability to make judgments on, 87–89

suffering of animals and, 83–85, 113–14

using violence undermines, 121–22

utilitarian approach to, 100

animal rights
animal rights advocates on, 31, 79–80

animals have no claim to, 33–34

applied to the real world, 80–81

argument for, 125–26

arguments against, problems with, 36–37

biological rights and, 37–38

capacity for suffering and, 42–43

danger to humans when respecting, 56–57

debate over human rights *vs.,* 21

human morality approves, 21–22

as independent of welfare to humans, 40–42

must be condemned, 58

philosophy of
is compassionate, 25–26
is individually fulfilling, 26–27

is just, 25

is peace-loving, 27–28

is scientific, 24

is socially progressive, 26–27

is unprejudiced, 24–25

is unselfish, 26

the soul and, 38–39

animal rights activists
on animal cloning, 175

on animal experimentation, 18

on animal rights, 31, 56–57, 79–80

are falsely labeled as terrorists, 60–63

conflicting ethical views with animal research community, 119–20

criminal charges against, 17, 18–19, 60

extreme tactics by, 57

protests against toxicity tests by, 15–16

violence and intimidation by, 14–15, 55, 126
concerns over, 15
effectiveness of non-violence and, 121–22
is silencing the scientific community, 65–67
legislation to curb, 16–17
punishment should be given for, 57–58
scientific community must speak out about, 67–68
undermines ethical basis of animal rights movement, 121

animals
act without conscience, 31

are biologically similar to humans, 140

are equal to humans, 28

are not little persons, 78

attacks on humans by wild, 30–31

care and treatment of research, 136–37

differences between humans and
  ability to feel pain and, 47–48
  changing notions of, 46–48
  consciousness and, 48–49
  crossing the species barrier and, 51–53
  evolution and, 49–50
  in moral and mental stature, 31–33, 50
  speciesism and, 77–78

have a fixed value, 32

humans are the chief threat to welfare of, 116–17

humans have greater value than, problem with, 91–92

humans' responsibility to, 79

it is wrong to prioritize humans over, 43

kill each other, 39–40

reasons biomedical research uses, 140–41

regulation improving welfare of, 80

value of animal research for, 128, 142–43

see also cloning, animal; primates

Animal Scientific Procedures Act (1986), 87

animal-to-human transplants
  for AIDS patients, 154
  animal suffering with, 180–81
  benefits of transgenic clones and, 200–201
  better organs with, 183–85
  cost savings with, 185
  danger of viral diseases from, 180, 181
  human desire for longevity and, 178, 181
  need for, 183

Animal Welfare Act (AWA), 136, 137, 143, 155

apes, 111–13

Appleton, Josie, 44

Aquinas, Thomas, 50

Archibald, Kathy, 157, 162

Aristotle, 50

Aziz, Tipu, 17

baboon bone marrow transplants, 154

Ball, Matt, 35

Bateson, Patrick, 124

Baxter, Greg, 167, 170, 171

Baycol, 162

BCG vaccine, 106

Bentham, Jeremy, 30, 92, 114, 120

Bio (web site organization), 175

biomedical research
  cloned livestock and, 178
  contemporary animal experimentation for, 146–47
  failure of animal experimentation for, 145–46
  helping animals, 142–43
  humans are equally vital to, 141
  for new drug development, 141–42
  non-human primates are required for, 104–107
  reasons animals are used for, 140–41
  redirecting funds from animal research and, 151
  scientific limitations on animal model for, 149–51
  there is no alternative to using animals for, 154, 156
  see also medical progress; prescription drugs

biotechnology. *See* cloning, animal; genetically modified animals

Bloom, Steve, 14, 66

British Union for Abolition of Vivisection (BUAV), 85, 149

Bross, Irwin, 161

Buddhism, 116

Burden Neurological Institute (England), 90

Bush, George W., 60

Cambridge University, 15, 55, 113

cancer research, 145–46, 146–47, 202

Cavalieri, Paola, 47

cell-culture testing, 168

Center for Food Safety and Applied Nutrition, 155

central nervous system biology and disease, 107

Childe, V. Gordon, 49

Christianity, 47, 114, 116, 120

civil disobedience, 121–22

cloning, animal
    animal welfare concerns with, 207–208
    benefits of, 200–202
    cattle, 175–76
    examples of, 205–206
    of farm animals, problems with, 206–207
    nuclear transfer process for, 198–99
    opposition to, 175
    for pets, 205
    transgenic proteins from, 199–200
    viral dangers of animal-to-human transplants and, 179

Coalition for Medical Progress (CMP), 85

Coetzee, J.M., 111

compassion, 25–26

computer-based medical research, 156, 163

Conniff, Richard, 74

conscience, animals act without, 31

consciousness, human, 48–49

Cornell University, 170, 171

cows, 175–76, 191, 208

Crawford, Lester, 194

Cyagra, 208

Darley Oaks Farm (England), 14, 65, 67

Darwin, Charles, 120

Darwinism, 50–51, 116

Dawkins, Richard, 93

deontological approach, 98, 100

Derbyshire, Stuart, 32

DeRose, Chris, 56

Descartes, René, 83–84

diabetes, 140

Di Beradino, Marie A., 197

Ding, Erwin, 100

dissection, in the classroom, 71–72

DNA, 48, 199–200

Dolly (cloned sheep), 198, 205–206

drugs. *See* prescription drugs

Druyan, Ann, 42

D'Silva, Joyce, 177

Economist (magazine), 14–15

Edmunds, Malcolm, 130

empathy, 100

Enlightenment philosophers, 46, 47

environment, philosphy of animal rights protects, 27

epilepsy, animal research on, 140–41

Epstein, Alex, 54

Eraldin, 162

ethics, of animal cloning, 203
    see also animal research, ethics
        and justification of
European Patent Convention, 84
European Patent Directive, 84
European Union (EU), 84
evolution, 49–50, 116–17

farm animals, cloning, 206–207
Feinberg, Mark, 115
Ferrier, David, 99
Festing, Simon, 66–67
Food and Drug Administration
    (FDA), 155, 194, 206, 208
food, cloned animals for, 206–207
Fouassier, Alexandre, 186
Fox, Fiona, 64
Freedman, David H., 165
Freedom of Information (FOI)
    Act, 89

Gallagher, J., 161
genetically modified animals, 176
    animal suffering and, 84
    choice of animal and protein
        for, 189
    cost savings with organs from,
        185
    for food, FDA on, 194
    inconsistent results with,
        193–95
    is a cost-effective option,
        189–90
    opportunities with, 187–88
    procedure methods for,
        188–89
    unknown dangers of pharm-
        ing and, 195–96
    used for human antibodies,
        191
    viral dangers of animal-to-
        human transplants and, 17
genetic diseases, research on, 148

Genetic Savings and Clone, 175,
    205
Ginzburg, Vitaly L., 31–32
Glaxo-SmithKline (GSK), 85
Goodall, Jane, 51
Graham, David, 150
Gray, John, 110
Greek, Ray, 115
Griffith, Linda, 167

Hammond, Gladys, 15
Handbook of Laboratory Animal
    Science, 160
Harlowe, Harry, 148
Helsinki Declaration, 94, 95, 97,
    98
Hematech, 191
hepatitis, 106–107
hormone replacement therapy
    research, 150, 159
Horn, Roy, 30
Hospital Doctor (magazine), 17
Howe, Sharon, 18
Hubel, David, 156
humanist perspective, 116
human rights
    animal rights independent
        from welfare for, 40–42
    being valued by other hu-
        mans, 37
    biological rights and, 37–38
    differences in degrees between
        animal rights and, 36–37
    the soul and, 38–39
    sources of, 33–34
humans
    animal research is justified by
        obligation to, 75–76
    animals are biologically simi-
        lar to, 140
    animals are equal to, 28
    are equally vital to medical
        research, 141

are not superior to other humans, 24–25
drive to survive, 74–75
experiments on
  are comparable to animal experimentation, 90–93
  consent and, 90, 94–95, 97–98, 99, 113–14
genetic differences between chimpanzees and, 25
have an obligation to animals, 79
have greater value than animals, problem with, 91–92
organ donations from, 183–84, 185
primate research results cannot be extrapolated to, 115
religious beliefs of, impacting view on animals, 114, 116
respecting animal rights is dangerous to, 56–57
similarity between apes and, 112–13
used in clinical trials for drug testing, 162–63, 164
wild animals attacking, 30–31
see also animals, differences between humans and; animal-to-human transplants; speciesism
Hume, David, 86
Huntingdon Life Sciences (HLS)
  Coalition for Medical Progress and, 85
  extreme tactics used against, 57, 65
  protests against, 15–16, 17, 55
  violence and intimidation against, 60, 65
Hurel, 167, 171
Hurley, Jennifer A., 152

immune-based diseases, 107
Interagency Coordinating Committee on the Validation of Alternative Methods (ICCVAM), 155

in vitro testing methods, 154, 156, 163
Isoprenaline, 162

Johnson, Daniel, 56
Johnson & Johnson, 171
justice, 25

Kafka, Franz, 111
Kant, Immanuel, 46
Kefauver-Harris Act (1961), 161
King, Martin Luther, 121–22
Kirin Brewery, 191
kittens, cloned, 205
Kjonaas, Kevin, 17, 18
Klausner, Richard, 159
Köhler, Wolfgang, 111–12, 117

Leaf, Clinton, 147
Leggett, Anthony J., 31–32
legislation. *See* regulation
Lewis, John, 17
Life Sciences Research, 65
Little, Clarence, 145
Lives of Animals, The (Coetzee), 111

macaques, 42–43
Machan, Tibor, 21, 50
malaria, 105–106
Manufacturing Chemist, 186
Market & Opinion Research International (MORI), 85
Marks, Jonathan, 52
McGowan, Megan, 62
meat eating, 123
media
  likening animal activists to, 119
  scientists are not speaking out about animal research in, 65–66

medical progress

    animal experimentation is vital to, 52, 55–56, 143, 152–54, 156

        con, 145–51

    debate on animal experimentation's contribution to, 17–18, 137

    disease prevention and, 139–40

    genetically modified animals are beneficial to, 189–91

        con, 193–96

    justifies animal research, 74–76

    through primate research, 104–107, 108

    through transgenic cloning, 200–203

Medical Research Modernization Committee, 150

Medicines Act (1968), 161

Mellanby, Kenneth, 100

Mental Health Act (1983), 95

Mercer, Ilana, 29

microdose studies, 164

morality

    Darwinism and, 50

    human, approving the concept of animal rights, 21–22

    in primates, 42–43

moral worth

    ability to feel pain defining, 47–48

    animals do not have, 31–33

    humans are different from animals in, 50

Morrison, Adrian R., 73

multiple sclerosis, 107

Murray, Joseph E., 56, 154

My Friend Flicka (O'Hara), 79

National Academy of Sciences, 195

National Association of Biology Teachers (NABT), 71

National Toxicology Program Interagency Center for the Evaluation of Alternative Toxicological Methods (NICEATM), 155

Nazi experiments, 90, 92, 100, 113

New England Anti-Vivisection Society (NEAVS), 71

Nobel Prize winners, 31–32

nonconsensual experiments, 95, 96–98, 99, 100

Norris, Jack, 35

North Carolina Association for Biomedical Research, 136

Nuremberg Code, 94, 97, 100

obesity, 140

O'Hara, Mary, 79

Opren, 162

O'Reilly, Bill, 30

Oxford University, 15, 67, 119

Pacelle, Wayne, 204

painience, 47

pain, moral worth defined by ability to feel, 47–48

Parkinson's Disease (PD), 141

peace, philosphy of animal rights and, 27

penicillin, 160

People for the Ethical Treatment of Animals, 56

pet cloning, 205

pharming, 195–96

pigs

    quality of organs from, 183–85

    viral dangers of transplants from, 179, 180

polio vaccine, 146, 153, 160

Political Animal: The Conquest of Speciesism, The (Ryder), 45

Polly (sheep), 200
Potter, Will, 59
prescription drugs
　animal's role in development
　　of new, 141–42
　animals used for research on
　　alternatives are available
　　　to, 163–64
　　to avoid expense of clini-
　　　cal trials, 162–63
　　failure of, 150–51
　　is done to satisfy govern-
　　　ment regulators, 161
　　is unreliable, 158–60
　deaths from side effects of,
　　158
　killing humans after being
　　pronounced safe, 162
　microchip technologies for
　　testing, 166–72
　using humans for clinical
　　trials on, 162–63, 164
primates
　humans are not different
　　from, 25
　kinship with, 51
　morality in, 42–43
　as source animals for trans-
　　plants, 181
　used for research
　　for AIDS, 147
　　cannot be extrapolated to
　　　humans, 115
　　capacity for suffering and,
　　　113–14
　　failure of alternatives to,
　　　107, 109
　　justifying, 103
　　medical necessity of, 104–
　　　107, 108
　　similarity between apes
　　　and humans and, 112–13
　　to study mental powers of
　　　apes, 111–12
Propulsid, 162

Prussian Academy, 111–12
psychological animal experiments,
　147–48
Public Health Service Policy of
　Humane Care and Use of Labo-
　ratory Animals, 155
Purdy, Laura, 180

rabbits, transgenic, 187, 189–90
Rafferty, Mary, 99
rationality
　animals do not possess,
　　32–33
　ethics of animal research and,
　　86–87
　evolution and, 50
Ravelingien, A., 184
Regan, Tom, 23, 74–75, 125–26
regulation
　allowing oversight commit-
　　tees to inspect animal re
　　search facilities and policies,
　　136–37
　of animal research, 143
　animal tests are done to sat-
　　isfy government, 161
　to avoid unnecessary animal
　　suffering, 103
　to curb intimidation cam-
　　paigns, 16–17
　ethical judgment is at the
　　heart of, 88–89
　going beyond reasonable de-
　　mands, 80
religious belief, 114, 116
"Report to an Academy, A"
　(Kafka), 111
Research Defence Society (RDS),
　85
Reynolds, Jack, 167–68
Rezulin, 162
rights, concept of
　under the Golden Rule, 38
　responsibility and, 93

suffering is the criterion for, 40–41

see also animal rights; human rights

Robl, Jim, 176, 191

Robson, John, 33

Royal Society for the Prevention of Cruelty to Animals, 100

Ryder, Richard
on ability to feel pain, 47
on Darwinism, 50
on exclusionary attitudes, 45
speciesism and, 93

Sabin, Albert, 153, 160

Sagan, Carl, 42

Schardein, James, 160

Schweitzer, Albert, 100

Science Media Centre (London), 65, 66

Scientific Steering Committee of the European Commission, 102

scientists. *See* animal research community

Scott, Gale, 182

secular humanists, 116

sentience, 47

Serious Organised Crime and Police Act, 16

sheep
cloned, 198, 205–206
transgenic, 188

Shuler, Michael, 166, 167, 168–70, 171, 172

Singer, Peter, 118
on ability to feel pain, 46, 47
on animal rights, 30
on differences between humans and animals, 25
on protection of non-human life, 76–77
on speciesism, 45, 77–78

Smith, Adam, 86

Smith, Wesley J., 57

Smy, Janis, 66

soul, the, 38–39

speciesism, 25, 45, 77–78, 93, 120

Stop Huntingdom Animal Cruelty (SHAC), 16, 17, 18–19, 61–62

Stop Huntingdom Animal Cruelty (website), 14

suffering
with animal-to-human transplants, 180–81
assessing animal, 132
as the criterion for granting rights, 40–41
ethics of animal research and, 83–85, 113–14
is unethical unless it benefits the patient, 127
primate research and, 113–14

syphilis experiments, 90

Takayama, Shuichi, 167

terrorists
animal rights activists are, 57–58
con, 60–63
media likening animal activists to, 119

thalidomide tragedy, 160, 161

Thomas, David, 82

toxicity testing, 148–49, 193

"Tracey" (transgenic sheep), 188

transgenic animals. *See* genetically modified animals

Treadwell, Timothy, 30

tuberculosis, 106

Tufts University Center for the Study of Drug Development, 167

United Kingdom
animal activist violence in, 119
animal rights protests in, 15–16

government is on side of animal researchers in, 85
legislation to curb intimidation campaigns in, 16–17
U.S. Department of Agriculture, 122
U.S. Food and Drug Administration, 175
U.S. Office for Naval Research, 90
U.S. Public Health Service Act, 143
utilitarianism, 100

Victims of Animal Rights Extremism, 16

Vioxx, 150–51, 162
vivisection, 71–72, 86, 89
Vlasak, Jerry, 119

Waite, Terry, 84
War on Terrorism, 60–61, 62
Wicklund, Freeman, 56
Wilson, E.O., 51
World War II, 90, 113

xenotransplantation. *See* animal-to-human transplants